MOLLY MAE FORCE

MASHUP MADNESS

HISTORY MADE FUN THROUGH PAST AND PRESENT ICONS

MASHUP MADNESS
HISTORY MADE FUN THROUGH PAST AND PRESENT ICONS

BY MOLLY MAE FORCE

ISBN 13: 978-1-944027-00-1

net worlding
PUBLISHING

Table of Contents

PREFACE

When I started my internship at Networlding with Melissa G Wilson as my mentor, I had no idea what to expect. I thought I would be sitting in a cubicle, reading and editing stories eight hours a day. I was very wrong. Instead, I published my own book. I still can't believe it! Melissa came to me with the idea to do mashups of past and present icons in blog posts. The blog posts soon turned into this book, a compilation of all the comparisons I explored. I learned so much writing this book from all the research that went into creating it. I had no idea that Thomas Edison was unpopular in school or that George Washington privately opposed slavery. Writing this book gave me so much more knowledge about history and I was pleasantly surprised to find myself enjoying it. That's what I hope my readers will get out of this, especially those that once found history dreadfully boring.

I know my dad hates when I say this because he's such a history buff, but my least favorite class in school was easily history. I didn't get anything out of it and I honestly counted down the minutes until it was over. The textbooks were dull and the homework assignments were even more uninteresting. I want kids to be fascinated history and even more by reading. I want kids to discover that thirst to read more and read often. I can only hope my book will help in some small way with that. I also want them to realize, as I have, that these historical figures were real people too. Harry Truman was an immense momma's boy and Princess Diana really struggled in school. These people are not just prominent figures to gawk at. That's what I love about finding the quirky facts about these individuals, there's a realness to them we can all relate to.

Acknowledgments

I'd like to express my colossal gratitude to Melissa G Wilson for making this possible and giving me the freedom to write this by myself. I never thought I'd get an opportunity like this. I'd also like to thank my parents for listening to me rant about how cool the people in this book are and for never failing to support me throughout my whole life. I'd also like to thank my incredible high school English teachers, Jane LaBond and Sharan Nayak for helping me realize my love of literature and writing.

1

ANDREW CARNEGIE TO ANDREW GARFIELD

Andrew Carnegie was a Scottish-American industrialist who was a forerunner in the American steel industry in the late nineteenth century. He is known as the second richest man in the world, behind only John D. Rockefeller. He is considered by many to be the father of American philanthropy, and after retiring from Carnegie Steel Company, which made him his fortune, he devoted the rest of his life giving his fortune away.

Andrew Garfield is an English-American actor who has earned international attention with his roles in *The Social Network*, for which he received Golden Globe and British Academy Film Award (BAFTA) nominations, and *The Amazing Spider-Man*, which was very well received. At age 31, Garfield is a rising star in the film industry and a well-known heartthrob.

These two have both influenced America and become a part of our American culture, but they actually **grew up in the UK**. Carnegie was born in Dunfermline, Scotland, and lived in a small cottage with his family. Their main room acted as a living room, dining room, and bedroom. When Carnegie

---

was thirteen, his father's weaving business was failing and the country was starving, so their family moved to the United States. They settled in Allegheny, Pennsylvania, an area rich in products for wool and cotton cloth. Allegheny is where Carnegie got his first job as a bobbin boy, changing spools of thread twelve hours a day for $1.20 a week. Garfield was born in Los Angeles, California, but he was raised in the town of Epsom, Surrey, a county in South East of England. He grew up going to school in England and attended the University of London, where he graduated in 2004. Garfield worked in theater and TV in England before his American film debut.

Carnegie and Garfield are two men who knew what they wanted to do with their lives starting at a young age. They both **started working toward their goals as children**. Carnegie, after getting his first job as a bobbin boy, went to work as a telegraph messenger for the Pittsburg Office of the Ohio Telegraph Company for a whopping $2.50 a week. (No thanks.) This job came with benefits, such as free admission to the local theater where Carnegie could watch Shakespeare, whom he ending up developing an appreciation for. He knew that he wanted to move up in the industry and worked very hard by memorizing the locations of all of Pittsburgh's businesses and the faces of important men, making many connections this way. Within a year, he was promoted to be an operator, and by age eighteen, he was hired to be a superintendent of the Pittsburgh Division of Pennsylvania Railroad Company.

Garfield might not have moved his way up the business ladder as a boy, but he did become focused on his dreams. He started acting classes when he was just twelve and appeared in youth theater productions. He won awards for his stage acting and made his British television debut in 2005 in a teen drama called *Sugar Rush*. From this, he gained attention and landed a role in two episodes of England's famous BBC show, *Doctor Who*, in 2007. He was named in *Variety*'s "10 Actors to Watch" after these appearances, and boy, were they right. Garfield gained good review after good review for his acting and has started to get noticed in Hollywood.

Andrew Carnegie and Garfield may have started young in their careers, but it wasn't until **age twenty-six when they both first got their big break**. In 1861, during the Civil War, Carnegie was appointed as the superintendent of the Military Railways and the Union Government's telegraph lines in the East at age twenty-six. He used the railroads to deliver ammunition to the Union troops. Under his authority, the telegraph service assisted the Union cause, which led to an eventual victory. He left the railroad company after the war, but his connections to its management led to his success in the ironworks trade where he started making the big bucks.

In 2010, at age twenty-six, Garfield co-starred in *The Social Network*, a drama based on the creators of Facebook. Critics and viewers received his performance very well, earning him wider recognition in the American film industry. *Rolling Stone* magazine said about his performance, "Keep your eyes on Garfield—he's shatteringly good, the soul of a film that might otherwise be without one." Also, in 2010, he was cast in his first starring role as Spider-Man alongside actress Emma Stone in *The Amazing Spider-Man*. Boo-yah!

Though these men could use their success only toward their own benefit, they chose not to. They have both done considerable **charity work**. Carnegie believed that using his fortune to benefit others rather than just making money for himself was important. He thought that no one needed more than $50,000 a year and didn't need to increase his fortune more than that. In his book, *The Gospel of Wealth*, he says that the rich have "a moral obligation to distribute [their money] in ways that promote the welfare and happiness of the common man" and "The man who dies thus rich, dies disgraced." Carnegie gave an estimated $350 million, almost 90 percent of his entire wealth, to his philanthropic causes. He felt strongly about literature and education, giving most of his fortune to build more than 2,500 public libraries and to fund research in science, education, and world peace. He also was a fan of the arts and gave $1.1 million to construct the legendary Carnegie Hall concert venue in New York. He once offered to give the Philippines $20 million so the country could buy its independence.

Garfield shares a passion for giving and is a known supporter of many charities, including Small Steps Project, Stand Up to Cancer, Starlight Children's Foundation, and Worldwide Orphans Foundation, for which he is an ambassador. He and girlfriend Emma Stone are known for using paparazzi photos to the advantage of charities by holding up signs of organizations to contribute to when they are bombarded with cameras.

2

ANNE FRANK TO ANNE HATHAWAY

Anne Frank is one of the most inspirational people the world has ever known. Her diary, documenting her time in hiding as a young Jewish girl during the Holocaust, is one of the most widely read books, published in more than sixty languages. It has become a required read in many school curriculums and a tool for teaching the world what hope really looks like.

Anne Hathaway is an American actor, singer, and producer who is adored by millions of fans and respected in the Hollywood community as one of their finest actresses. She has won both Academy and Golden Globe Awards for her performances. You may know her as the hilarious Mia Thermopolis in *The Princess Diaries* or the awkward and lovable Andrea in *The Devil Wears Prada*. She has also starred in films such as *Interstellar*, *The Dark Knight Rises*, and *Les Misérables*.

Anne Frank was born as a German citizen in Frankfurt, Germany. In 1941, because of anti-Semitism and the beginning of the Holocaust, she lost her German citizenship. Turns out both Anne Frank and Anne Hathaway have **German roots**. Hathaway has mostly Irish and French ancestry, but she and her family also have distant German lineage.

Anne Frank and Anne Hathaway both have connections to **Judaism**. Frank was raised as a liberal Jew and did not observe all of the customs and traditions of Judaism. Before going into hiding, Frank and her family lived in an assimilated community of Jewish and non-Jewish citizens. Even though her family moved out of Germany to the Netherlands, the Germans invaded the Netherlands and began segregating, as well as persecuting, Jews. Tragically, her family was found while in hiding, and they were sent to a concentration camp.

Anne Hathaway was raised strictly Catholic and even heavily considered becoming a nun at age eleven. However, at age fifteen, her brother came out to her family as gay, and she separated herself from Catholicism, unable to support a religion that didn't support her brother. Hathaway's connection to Judaism comes from her marriage to a Jewish man, Adam Shulman. The couple was married in 2012 with an interfaith Roman Catholic and Jewish service.

From a young age, both Frank and Hathaway had **dreams of being an actress**. Frank wrote in her diary about how she longed to be an actress because she loved watching movies. She even glued movie star photographs to her wall, which can be seen at The Anne Frank House. Sadly, Jewish people were forbidden from attending the movie theaters starting in 1941.

Anne Hathaway's mother, Kate, is an actress and inspired her daughter to become one as well. Kate played Fantine in the first US tour of *Le Misérables* in addition to other roles. Hathaway, unlike Frank, was able to follow out her dreams and is now one of the most famous and beloved actresses in Hollywood.

A charming common thread between these famous girls is **Shakespeare**. Frank loved quoting Shakespeare and found his work powerful in its themes of love, happiness, and justice. Hathaway's parents decided to name their daughter after Shakespeare's wife, Anne Hathaway. She also appeared as Viola in the New York Shakespeare Festival's summer 2009 *Twelfth Night* production.

Anne Frank excelled early on in reading and writing as a student. She wrote very frequently and became a well-known writer after her diary was published. She's hailed as a remarkable writer for her young age, wisely commenting on WWII, the Holocaust, and the human experience. It looks like Frank isn't the only one interested in **reading and writing**. Hathaway also loves to read great literature and, though she isn't a writer, she appreciates good writing. Her favorite book is *The Fountainhead* by Ayn Rand. Hathaway has even said that if her acting career hadn't worked out, she wanted to be an English teacher.

Both Anne Frank and Hathaway **support women's rights**. Anne Frank has many famous quotes detailing her belief that everyone has some goodness within them and the utmost importance of having hope. Another lesser-known theme in Frank's diary is one that supports women's rights and equality. One of these quotes is,

"Women should be respected as well! Generally speaking, men are held in great esteem in all parts of the world, so why shouldn't women have their share? Soldiers and war heroes are honored and commemorated, explorers are granted immortal fame, martyrs are revered, but how many people look upon women too as soldiers? Women, who struggle and suffer pain to ensure the continuation of the human race, make much tougher and more courageous soldiers than all those big-mouthed freedom-fighting heroes put together!"

Seems like Anne Frank was a feminist! Anne Hathaway is one, too. She's a women's rights honoree in both *Elle* magazine's "Women in Hollywood" tribute and The Step Up Women's Network, which is a nonprofit membership organization dedicated to supporting, connecting, and advancing women and girls.

3

Ben Franklin to Ben & Jerry

Ben Franklin is one of those Founding Father guys. He had a lot of talents, including being an author, political theorist, politician, inventor, scientist, and diplomat. He's called "The First American" for his early campaigning for separation from England. He is considered America's hypothetical first president because he played the leading role in our nation's creation. He was a signer of both the Declaration of Independence and the Constitution. Now, his face adorns our $100 bills and can be seen on monuments all across the US.

Ben & Jerry's has that ice cream, frozen yogurt, and sorbet that's so hard to say no to. When thinking of the famously-known Founding Father Ben Franklin, ice cream doesn't usually come to mind. However, the founding fathers of great tasting ice cream Ben & Jerry have more in common with him than you think.

Franklin as well as Ben & Jerry got their start in the state of **Pennsylvania**. This is the state where one seventeen-year-old Franklin ran away to in order to make a new start for himself in Philadelphia. He began working in printer shops, became publisher of *The Pennsylvania Gazette*, and eventually became a well-known author. Then, of course, he was on the legendary Committee of Five that drafted The Declaration of Independence, all in the state of Pennsylvania. This is also the state where young Ben Cohen and Jerry Greenfield, both twenty-six, completed a $5 correspondence course on ice cream at Penn State University. One year later, they invested $12,000 for their very own ice cream shop. The rest is history!

We can also agree that Ben Franklin and Ben & Jerry are known for their game-changing **inventions**. Franklin made major strides with electricity, being the first to discover positive and negative electric charges. He is best known for proving lightning was a source of electricity by flying a kite in a storm. This experiment also led to his invention of the lightning rod, used to protect buildings and houses from lightning strikes. Ben & Jerry didn't invent electricity, but they did invent amazing ice cream. Their creation is well known for their chunks of flavor as well as many original flavors. To name a few, there's Chunky Monkey, containing banana ice cream, chocolate chunks, and walnuts; there's Phish Food, made with chocolate ice cream, chocolate and marshmallow chunks, and caramel; and there's Peace of Cake, made with strawberry cheesecake ice cream with chunks of strawberry and cookie swirls. Yummmm.

Another parallel between Ben Franklin and Ben & Jerry has to do with their involvement with **social action and human rights in America**. Other than his involvement in the Declaration, Franklin was a fierce fighter against racial prejudice. From organizing protection for American Indians to taking on the role of an abolitionist and freeing many slaves, it's clear Franklin wanted freedom for all Americans. Ben & Jerry follow his example by supporting equal marriage rights for same-sex couples with the names of their ice cream flavors, such as changing Chubby Hubby to Hubby Hubby in celebration of Vermont legalizing same-sex marriage.

Ben Franklin and Ben & Jerry are linked by their commitment to the **bettering of the community and the general public**. Ben Franklin helped the community by taking part in educating the youth of Pennsylvania by assisting in the startup of schools as well as creating a plan for American colleges. He founded the American Philosophical Society to help scientific men with their discoveries. He also had major involvement in the establishment of Pennsylvania Hospital, the first hospital in the US. He became a member of the Society for the Encouragement of the Arts, Manufactures & Commerce, dedicated to furthering the creation of science and art. The Ben & Jerry Foundation is dedicated to funding community-oriented projects. They are involved with the Children's Defense Fund in order to convince Congress to bring children's most basic needs into the national agenda. To support farmers and get them the fair price for their harvest, Ben & Jerry participate in Fair Trade efforts. They also participated in a protest against oil drilling in the Arctic National Wildlife Refuge. In addition to helping people and animals, Ben & Jerry help the Earth by partnering with SaveOurEnvironment.org to fight global warming.

4

BETSY ROSS TO BETTY WHITE

Betsy Ross is the woman credited with making the first American flag in 1776, after a visit from George Washington and a small committee. When George Washington shows up and asks you to make a flag for America, you do it. The "Betsy Ross Flag" contains thirteen stars and stripes after the thirteen original colonies. There isn't any archival evidence or records to prove this story of the first American flag, only the writings of her grandson in the 1870s documenting her story in a research paper for the Historical Society of Pennsylvania. Whether or not the story is true, historians aren't sure, but she sure is an important and well-known historical figure.

Betty White is an American actress, comedian, author, producer, radio host, singer, and TV personality. She is best known for her roles on the *Mary Tyler Moore Show* and *The Golden Girls*. She's had the longest TV career for a female entertainer, still a prominent figure in Hollywood at age ninety-three. She's known as a huge supporter of animal welfare and has donated tens of thousands of dollars to the Los Angeles Zoo and is a member of the board of directors.

Betsy Ross and Betty White were both known as beautiful young women, so it isn't a total surprise that they've both had **three husbands**. Betsy Ross first got married at age twenty-one to a fellow apprentice at an upholstering business, named John Ross, who was the son of an Anglican priest. Betsy Ross was split from her family and the Quaker congregation when the couple eloped in 1773. After her first husband died in the war, she was believed to be a "beautiful young widow" at the age of twenty-four, who distracted Hessian Colonel Carl von Donop. He kept his forces out of the crucial Battle of Trenton where the Hessians were defeated. Her second husband was a mariner named Joseph Ashburn who was charged with treason due to his British ancestry and died in British jail. Together, they had two daughters. Her third husband was John Claypoole, the man who informed her that her second husband had died. They had five daughters together. That's a lot of daughters!

Betty White didn't have any children, but she did get married three times. Her first marriage in 1945, when White was twenty-three, was to a US Army Air Corps pilot named Dick Barker. They got divorced that same year, and White married her second husband in 1947. His name was Lane Allen, and he was a Hollywood agent. That marriage lasted two years.

It wasn't until White was forty-one that she married her third husband, TV host and personality Allen Ludden. They met on the game show *Password* when she was the celebrity guest in 1961. Ludden proposed at least twice to White before she accepted. Looks like White knew how to play hard to get! After getting married, Ludden later died from stomach cancer in 1981, and White hasn't remarried since. When Larry King asked whether or not she wanted to remarry in an interview, White said, "Once you've had the best, who needs the rest?" Awww.

These two iconic women **lived during a major American war and contributed to war efforts**. Ross was only twenty-three when the American Revolutionary War broke out, and since she was in the upholstery business, she assisted in making needed supplies for Continental army soldiers. She repaired uniforms, made tents and blankets, and stuffed paper tube cartridges with musket balls for prepared packaged ammunition. White's war was World War II, during her initial rise to stardom. Because of WWII, she put her dreams to the side and joined the American Women's Voluntary Services. She spent time delivering supplies throughout the Hollywood Hills via a post exchange truck during the day, and at night, she spent time at dances thrown to give excitingly grand send-offs to soldiers set to ship out.

Ross and White are both **Christians**. Ross, after being expelled from the Quaker congregation after eloping with her first husband, turned to an Episcopal church called Christ Church. Another member of this church was soon-to-be-general George Washington. Betty White is a practicing member of Unity Church, described as a "positive, practical Christianity," which teaches the principles exemplified by Jesus Christ and promotes a life of health, prosperity, happiness, and peace of mind.

It isn't a secret that these two women represent a **symbol of women's contributions to American History**. Betsy Ross is the woman credited with creating the first American Flag. In 1776, a small committee including George Washington, Robert Morris, and relative George Ross came to Betsy and told her their need for a new American flag. Ross accepted the job and made some alterations to their design, including replacing their six-pointed stars for five-pointed ones. Ross is known as a patriotic symbol, someone who is a role model for young girls and an example of women's contributions to American history.

Betty White is a different kind of woman role model in America but an important one, nonetheless. She holds the Guinness World Record for having the longest TV career for a female entertainer. She is a pioneer of television, being one of the first women ever to have creative control both behind and in front of the camera. She's also recognized as the first woman to produce a sitcom. White has eighteen Emmy acting nominations and twenty-four Emmy nominations total, making her the second most nominated actress in Emmy history. White's first Emmy nomination was in 1950 for Best Actress on Television, the very first award and category in the Emmy history designated for women on TV. White is the only woman to have received an Emmy in all performing comedic categories and holds the record for longest span between Emmy nominations. Being a guest on many game shows over the years, she owns the title of the "First Lady of Game Shows" and is the first woman to receive an Emmy for Outstanding Game Show Host. You go, girl!

5

Bill Clinton to Bill Gates

Bill Clinton was the forty-second president of the United States and a member of the Democratic Party. Like most of our presidents, he is a very smart guy. He attended Georgetown, University of Oxford, and Yale Law School. Yale is where he met future wife and politician Hillary Clinton. While in office, he presided over the longest peacetime economic expansion and signed the North American Free Trade Agreement (NAFTA) into a law. Clinton left office with the highest approval rating from Americans since WWII, even though he is well known for the Monica Lewinsky scandal.

Bill Gates was the youngest self-made billionaire and now holds the title of the richest man in the world, with an estimated net worth of $78.9 billion. That's a lot of dough! His fortune came from co-founding Microsoft, still the world's largest PC software company. After serving as CEO and chief software architect at Microsoft, Gates quit to pursue philanthropy through The Bill & Melinda Gates Foundation. It is the largest private foundation in the world and seeks to globally improve healthcare and reduce poverty while expanding educational opportunities in America.

While Clinton is a politician and Gates is a computer nerd, they have both **written books**. Clinton has four books to his name including *Between Hope and History*, *My Life*, *Giving: How Each of Us Can Change the World*, and *Back to Work: Why We Need Smart Government for a Strong Economy*. *My Life* documents what it was like growing up as Bill Clinton and the lessons he learned from his family, which made him the man he became. The memoir is 1,008 pages and has been made fun of for its length. Jon Stewart, satirical news program host, once joked, "I have to confess, I did not finish the entire book; I'm on . . . page 12,000."

Gates has been the author of two books, *The Road Ahead* and *Business @ the Speed of Thought*. *The Road Ahead*, published in 1995, is a synopsis of the possible consequences of the PC revolution and a bright future due to digital communications systems. *Business @ the Speed of Thought* was published in 1999 and is a consideration of the ways in which technology and business are united. It also explains how using technology in business infrastructures and networks can give your business an edge over the competition.

These intelligent men were recognized for their smarts as **scholars**. Bill Clinton was the recipient of a Rhodes Scholarship, sending him to attend the University of Oxford in England. It is considered the most prestigious scholarship in the world, offering courses at the university to any full-time postgraduate who wants to continue their studies. Bill Gates was a National Merit Scholar at a private college prep school called the Lakeside School in Seattle, Washington. He earned a 1590 out of 1600 on the SAT and enrolled at Harvard but dropped out during his sophomore year in order to pursue the creation of the Microsoft business.

These famous dudes have both **stayed married to one wife**. Clinton, though he has faltered in his faithfulness to Hillary, has stayed married to her for over forty years. Hillary was one year ahead of Clinton at Yale, and after they met in 1971 at the Yale Law Library, they were quickly dating and inseparable. Clinton moved to California with Hillary and postponed plans to coordinate the George McGovern campaign for the 1972 presidential election. Clinton and Hillary married in 1975, and they had their daughter shortly after. Gates, after becoming famous for Microsoft and his fortune, was named one of "50 Most Eligible Bachelors" in 1985 by *Good Housekeeping.* He married his wife, Melinda, in 1994, and they had two daughters and one son. With Melinda, Gates founded The Bill & Melinda Gates Foundation in order to follow in the footsteps of Andrew Carnegie and John D. Rockefeller's philanthropy. Gates and his wife strongly believe in giving, creating the "Gates-Buffet Giving Pledge" as a commitment to donate at least half of their wealth overtime to charity.

Gates is definitely the computer guy, but they were both responsible for **Internet popularization**. The Clinton administration was the first to introduce the first official White House website, whitehouse.gov, in 1994. His administration was also intent on web-based communication, convincing the US court system and US military to utilize the Internet. With this encouragement, Americans were allowed more access to the US government through the Internet. The Federal Information Technology Executive Order was issued by Clinton to order the heads of all federal agencies to make use of the Internet to give the public more access to information. Of course, with Gate's invention of Microsoft Windows, the PC market boomed. Microsoft is the front-runner in Internet search and the video game industry.

6

Daniel Boone to Daniel Radcliffe

Daniel Boone, called "the founding father of westward expansion," is the most widely known American frontiersman. He is famous for his exploration and settlement of what is now Kentucky. He was also one of the first folk heroes of the United States, an iconic figure and subject of fiction that exaggerated details of his life. He's remembered as a hunter, pioneer, and "Indian-fighter" who has been made synonymous with the American outdoors. Author John Filson's "The Adventures of Colonel Daniel Boone" and Timothy Flint's *Biographical Memoir of Daniel Boone, the Fist Settler of Kentucky* embellished the events in Boone's life. They described him fighting hand-to-hand with a bear and escaping from Indians by swinging on vines. He fought in the American Revolutionary War against the Shawnee Indians, who were being helped by the British. Boone became a prisoner of the Shawnees but was adopted into their tribe to replace fallen warriors, allowing him to know their military plans. When he found out they would be attacking the village he founded in

Kentucky, called Boonesborough, he betrayed the Shawnees and escaped to warn his people.

Daniel Radcliffe is an English actor known worldwide as Harry Potter. He starred in the *Harry Potter* film series, which included eight movies over the span of ten years. His parents actually first refused the role for Radcliffe, unsettled by the fact that seven film shootings would occur in Los Angeles rather than the UK. Warner Bros. badly wanted Radcliffe to play the part, so they ended up drawing up a two-movie contract shot in the UK, which was accepted. Radcliffe became the complete embodiment of reader's imaginations, causing his fame and fortune to skyrocket.

Even though Boone is an American, he has English ancestry. In fact, both Boone and Radcliffe's **parents are from the UK**. The Boone family once belonged to the Quaker religion and was persecuted in England for their differing religious views. Boone's father emigrated from England to Pennsylvania, where he met Boone's mother who was also a Quaker originally from England. Radcliffe was born in West London to a Protestant father from Northern Ireland and a Jewish mother born in South Africa but raised in Essex, England.

Like many famous figures, these men realized their passions early on in life. Both Boone and Radcliffe had **started careers by age twelve**. Boone was given his first rifle at the age of twelve, giving him the responsibility to hunt for his family's food. He learned quickly from local settlers and became the skillful hunter folk tales described him to be. One story continuously told about Boone happened when he was a young boy hunting in the woods with some friends. A panther howled and leaped toward him. That's a scary situation to be in! Boone was able to shoot the cat through the heart before it could attack. The story became part of his popular image.

Daniel Radcliffe made his acting debut in the BBC's TV movie *David Copperfield* at age ten. *Harry Potter's* movie director, Chris Columbus, saw a clip of Radcliffe in the movie and immediately knew he was the one. J.K. Rowling saw the audition tape of Radcliffe and began to cry because she believed he was the complete manifestation of her Harry. Radcliffe was signed onto the *Harry Potter* films at age eleven and completed the first movie by age twelve. His role as the young wizard, Harry Potter, who went to school at Hogwarts School of Witchcraft and Wizardry brought major success to the franchise.

These men didn't carry on their parent's religious views and are both considered to be **nonreligious**. Two of Daniel Boone's siblings married outside the Quaker community, causing controversy. Boone's parents were compelled to publicly apologize, though they stood behind their children's decisions. Boone's brother and father were expelled from the

Quaker community, and Boone didn't attend church again. Throughout his life, he still identified as a Christian man and had his children baptized, but he didn't practice his religion.

Daniel Radcliffe is considered Jewish because of his mother, but he's actually a candid atheist. He claims that he's very comfortable being an atheist and doesn't approve of religion impacting legislation, though he doesn't preach about his atheist views.

7

Princess Diana to Diana Ross

Diana, Princess of Wales, is one of the most beloved historical figures to date. She was born into a family of British nobility but earned her royalty status when she married Charles, Prince of Wales. Princess Diana was praised for her charity work and her love of children. She's described as the "world's most photographed woman" and was adored by people around the globe for her beauty, compassion, and charisma. She died at age thirty-six after being fatally injured in a car crash while she was in Paris, fleeing from paparazzi. Her death was unexpected and created a worldwide mourning, with her funeral reaching British television's audience peak of 32.10 million viewers.

Diana Ross is one of the biggest icons in the music business and got her start in Detroit's Motown with The Supremes, one of the world's best-selling girl groups of all time. Ross even rivaled The Beatles in worldwide popularity, trailblazing as a successful African American R&B and soul artist. She was a mainstream success, and her classic songs continue to be played on the radio. Some of The Supremes' songs include, "Stop! In the Name of Love," "Baby Love," "Come See About Me," and "Someday We'll Be Together." As a solo artist, she continued to produce hits such as "Reach Out and Touch (Somebody's Hand)," "Ain't No Mountain High Enough," "I'm Coming Out," and "Endless Love." She has been named in the *Guinness Book of World Records* as the most successful female music artist in history with more hits than any female artist in the charts.

Diana Ross might be the artist of the two, but it's true that these women both **enjoy music and dancing**. In school growing up, Princess Diana struggled in her math and science classes and was considered a poor student, unable to pass the exams in England in order to receive her diploma and attend university. Diana excelled in music, specifically the piano, and enjoyed her training in classical ballet. Her dream was to become a professional ballerina at the prestigious Royal Ballet.

Diana Ross was the lead singer of The Supremes and then continued singing as a solo artist. She has appeared on Broadway and was named "Female Entertainer of the Century" by *Billboard* magazine. Ross has been nominated for twelve Grammys and was a recipient of the Kennedy Center Honors in 2007 for her success as an artist.

These two leading ladies weren't always the stars of the show. Actually, they each **started at low-paying jobs**. Princess Diana, before she was a princess, loved working with children and became a nursery assistant at the Young England School. Diana also worked as a nanny and a dance instructor for kids.

Diana Ross was talented in design and seamstress skills while in school and dreamed of being a fashion designer. Her first job was at Hudson's Department Store where she was actually the first African American employee allowed outside the kitchen. For extra income, in addition to working for Hudson's, Ross provided hairdressing services to her neighbors.

These beautiful women didn't stay with their husbands and both ended up getting **divorced** in their mid-thirties. Princess Diana's divorce from Prince Charles was highly publicized. Their thirteen-year age difference, incompatible personalities, and affairs led to their break-up. Diana revealed later that her husband constantly looked down on her, and she was very unhappy with him. They had two children together, William and Harry, who were the second and third in line to the throne. Diana died the year after her divorce, before she could remarry.

Diana Ross has been married twice and has five children: three girls and two boys. Ross's first marriage was to music executive Robert Ellis Silberstein. Their marriage lasted six years before falling apart. She remarried eight years later to a Norwegian billionaire named Arne Næss, Jr., who Ross considered the love of her life. Sadly, he died in a South African mountain climbing accident. She has not remarried.

You wouldn't think that these two incredible women had self-esteem issues, but the reality is that Princess Diana and Diana Ross struggled with **eating disorders and mental health problems**. Princess Diana suffered with the rejection of her husband and ended up lapsing into depression. Diana stated, "My husband made me feel inadequate in every possible way that each time I came up for air he pushed me down again." She revealed her depression and self-harming to the press, in addition to her eating disorder, bulimia nervosa. Biographers of Princess Diana suggest that she suffered from borderline personality disorder, meaning she was emotionally unstable in her behaviors, relationships, and self-image.

Diana Ross felt pressure from her music producer and his many demands, causing her to suffer from the eating disorder called anorexia nervosa. Ross also turned to drinking, which caused her to be admitted into a facility for drug and alcohol abuse because her children were concerned about their mother's health. Ross struggled from depression as well and relied on substances to get her through the day.

8

DOLLEY MADISON TO DOLLY PARTON

Dolley Madison was the wife and First Lady to President James Madison. She also performed First Lady duties for President Thomas Jefferson, who was then widowed. Madison is known for her social graces, hospitality, and grace. She defined the role of a First Lady by promoting her husband and gaining him popularity. She also helped furnish the newly built White House and is credited as a heroine for saving the classic portrait of George Washington when the British set fire to the White House in 1814.

Dolly Parton is an American singer–songwriter and actress who is known by everyone in the country music industry. She is also a known humanitarian and a supporter of the LGBT community. The Country Music Hall of Fame star has recorded over 3,000 songs in her career, known for songs such as "I Will Always Love You," "Jolene," "Coat of Many Colors," and "9 to 5." She is the most honored female country music performer in history, and is also famous for her plastic surgery. Parton has had twenty-five songs reach number one on the

Billboard country charts, a record for a female artist. She also has forty-one career top ten country albums, which is a record for any artist.

These women both come from **big families**. Dolley Madison, born Dolley Payne, was the first girl in her family and later had a total of seven siblings. Madison was born in New Garden, North Carolina, but she was raised on a plantation in Virginia. When Madison was in her twenties, her family moved to Philadelphia where she met her first husband, John Todd, with whom she started her own family.

Dolly Parton was born the fourth of twelve children in Tennessee. Parton grew up close to her grandfather, who was the preacher at their local church. Many of her first performances were in a church.

Speaking of churches, Madison and Parton are both **Christians**. Madison was raised as a Quaker, which was her mother's faith. Her father became a Quaker after marrying her mother, and he was among a group of Quakers against slavery who freed his slaves. Madison's first husband, John Todd, was a Quaker lawyer. Her second husband, James Madison, was not a Quaker. She was expelled from the Quaker religion for marrying someone who wasn't of the same religion. Parton is a devout Christian, raised in a religious family. She has said in interviews that God is a big part of her life, saying, "God is in everything I do, and all my work glorifies Him." Many of

Parton's songs, such as "Letter to Heaven" and "Hello God" reflect her religion. She has become an icon within the gay community for calling anti-gay Christians sinners.

These women might be famous for their lifestyles, but they weren't always living a lavish life. Both women **lived in poverty** at some point in their lives. Dolley Madison, after her husband's death, became very poor. As a widow in the last days of her existence, Madison lived in absolute poverty and struggled to get the bare necessities of life. A former slave of hers often lent her money so she could survive. In order to receive some money, she organized and copied James Madison's papers. She wished to sell her husband's seven volumes of papers, including his own notes on the 1787 convention, where the Constitution was created. Congress ended up buying the papers for $55,000.

Unlike Dolley Madison's poverty late in life, Dolly Parton started out dirt poor. Parton's family lived in a one-room cabin. Her father paid the doctor who delivered her with a bag of oatmeal. Like her religion, she has outlined her family's poverty in her music, in early songs such as "Coat of Many Colors" and "In the Good Old Days (When Times Were Bad)."

These women **didn't attend college**. Dolley Madison may have made a name for herself as the First Lady to James Madison, but you don't need to be educated to get that position. In fact, women didn't legally have access to college until 1848, the year before she died. Dolly Parton knew she wanted to be a singer from a very young age. She began performing as a child singing on local radio stations in Tennessee. At age eight, she received her first guitar. By age thirteen, she was recording music for Goldband Records and performing at the famous Grand Ole Opry alongside Johnny Cash. After graduating high school, she moved to Nashville and signed with Combine Publishing as a songwriter short-ly after arriving. She became a singer at age nineteen for Monument Records, where she was expected to become a bubblegum pop singer. But that wasn't her style. Parton was not happy with their decision and stuck to singing country music, eventually becoming a star.

9

FRANCIS BACON TO POPE FRANCIS

Francis Bacon is the man behind the scientific method, also known as the Baconian method, and is remembered for his work during the scientific revolution in the 1600s. Bacon is considered to be the father of empiricism, supporting the theory that all knowledge is gained from sense-experience. He was also a jurist, an expert in law, as well as an orator, a talented public speaker. Pope Francis is the 266th pope of the Catholic Church with a hugely favorable reputation, known as a relatable and down-to-earth guy. His nickname is "The People's Pope," and he has updated the Catholic Church's public image. He has focused on showing the church as a beacon of hope and comfort to those hurting, rather than focusing on the church's rules to police Catholics.

Though they both have made huge impacts in the world, they had humble beginnings. They both **started at low paying jobs** before gaining recognition. Francis Bacon attended Trinity College in Cambridge at the age of twelve and then traveled the world to study language and law. His father died suddenly when Bacon was eighteen, leaving him with little money and a future of debt. He sought a position at the English court to pursue his dreams of serving his country and church, but his application was denied. He went to work at Gray's Inn for two years to earn money before getting a junior position at the court.

Pope Francis was born in Buenos Aires, Argentina and graduated a technical secondary school with a chemical technician diploma. He worked for a few years in the foods section at a laboratory. Believe it or not, Pope Francis also worked as a bar bouncer as a young man. His other jobs included being a janitor, sweeping floors, and being a scientist, running tests in a chemical laboratory before joining the Jesuits.

Bacon and Francis have both assumed multiple **leadership positions** during their adult life. Bacon started his career as a parliamentarian at age twenty and progressed to being a bencher, a senior member position, and a reader, a position allowing legal lectures to be given. After being ordained as a Catholic priest, Pope Francis became Archbishop of Buenos Aires and then was named a cardinal in 2001. Francis was elected as pope in 2013, though he still dresses in traditional robes. Francis is a humble leader. While most popes of the Catholic Church wear lavish garments to show off their position of power and live in the Papal Palace, Francis wears plain robes lacking ornamentation and lives in a guesthouse near the Vatican that is filled with only the basic necessities.

These men are both known as **liberal-minded** leaders and have both **spoken against religious persecution**. Francis Bacon was open-minded toward the reform and simplification of the law. He opposed dictatorial powers and voiced his distain for punishment over differing religions. He also advocated for the unification of England and Scotland, significantly influencing the creation of the United Kingdom. Bacon was known as a tenderhearted judge in the courtroom, looking upon people with pity and compassion, free from vindictiveness.

Pope Francis is also known as liberal and tenderhearted, with his multiple examples of acceptance toward the poor and toward animals. Francis has shaken up the Catholic Church by stressing the importance of being open and welcoming. He is especially famous for the words he has spoken about the LGBT community. The quote, "If someone is gay and seeks the Lord with good will, who am I to judge?" was a huge step forward for the Catholic Church. The American LGBT magazine, *The Advocate*, named Pope Francis their Person of the Year for 2013. Pope Francis has also showed a liberal and forward-thinking attitude toward women of the Catholic Church. Francis has stated that women have much importance in the church, for they have a special role in spreading faith to their children and grandchildren. He has also recognized that although the first witnesses of Jesus's resurrection were women, their significance was ignored because, at the time, Jewish law only recognized males as credible witnesses. Like Bacon, he has condemned the persecution of religious minorities, specifically in Iraq, and calls for peace between religions, stating that each person sees the world in their own way. Acceptance of everyone, no matter what religion they practice, is important to both of these men.

10

GEORGE WASHINGTON TO GEORGE CLOONEY

George Washington, "The Founder of his Country," is a widely respected Founding Father and a monumental historical icon for America. He was our nation's first president, considered by many to be our nation's greatest president. He was also the commander-in-chief of the Continental army during the American Revolutionary War. In addition, he was the position of authority at the convention where the Constitution was drafted.

George Clooney is a strikingly handsome actor, a man adored by women of all ages who can be recognized by anyone even remotely engaged in pop culture. He has appeared in movies such as *Ocean's Eleven*, *Up in the Air*, *The Descendants*, and *Argo*. Needless to say, these two Georges are very different, but surprisingly, they have some things in common.

Washington and Clooney each share the honor of being named as *Time* **magazine's 100 Most Influential People** in the World. Washington was a part of *Time*'s book *The*

100 Most Influential People of All Time, which profiles great leaders and icons throughout history. Clooney was a part of *Times*'s 100 Most Influential People in the World in 2007, 2008, and 2009.

Though neither of them was born in **Ohio**, Washington and Clooney also each have a connection to the state. Washington's brother Lawrence was part of the Ohio Company, interested in settling on Ohio's land where the French were currently residing. Therefore, when Washington was a teenager, he was able to meet Robert Dinwiddie, the lieutenant governor of Virginia. He offered Washington a position in the Virginia militia and gave him the responsibility of delivering a letter to the French, asking them to leave the Ohio Valley. The French and Indian War started in the area of Ohio, and it was Washington's first experience with war. George Clooney didn't fight in the Ohio area, but he did spend much of his childhood there. Clooney attended schools in the cities of Columbus and then Mason, Ohio for elementary school and part of middle school.

Religion is something else these two iconic men have in common. Both Washington and Clooney were raised **Christian** and even participated as members of their church's board. Washington volunteered as a churchwarden, representing the members of the parish, and was able to cooperate with the priest. Clooney's family was very Catholic, and he served as an altar boy as a kid.

These men also seem to have had **two great loves** in their lives and both got **married at the age of twenty-eight**. Washington was only married once, to Martha Dandridge Custis, at age twenty-eight, but letters have revealed that he was in love with Sally Fairfax, the wife of his friend. George Washington was involved with two women, similar to George Clooney, who has had two wives. Though Clooney has been seen with many women, only two have stolen his heart to the point where they said their vows. Clooney married Talia Balsam when he was twenty-eight, and the marriage lasted four years. He got married again in 2014 to Amal Alamuddin when he was fifty-three.

Another interesting comparison between these two famous Georges is that **neither of them have children of their own**. When Washington married Martha, she already had two children from her previous marriage. Washington raised the children like they were his own. Together, Washington and Martha never had any children, which some suggest may be due to Washington's bad case of smallpox, which could have made him sterile. George Clooney, though married twice, hasn't taken the step to be a father. At the current age of fifty-four, it's unlikely he will ever have kids. But who knows, maybe him and Amal have upcoming plans for pregnancy!

A little-known fact about George Washington is that he was actually against slavery, an unpopular opinion for his time. Both Washington and Clooney have made strides toward **human rights**. Washington was actually the only Founding Father to put in his will and testament that he wanted his slaves to be freed. Not wanting to threaten the overall unity of the nation, Washington privately opposed slavery, thinking it both immoral and economically unreliable. Washington didn't sell his slaves during his lifetime because he didn't want to break up their families. To Robert Morris, a fellow Founding Father, Washington said, "There is not a man living who wishes more sincerely than I do, to see a plan adopted for the abolition of slavery." Clooney shows his support for human rights by supporting same-sex marriage. He participated in a play about legalizing same-sex marriage in California alongside Brad Pitt to raise money for The American Foundation for Equal Rights. He also contributes to the Gay, Lesbian, and Straight Education Network (GLSEN) to create a safe space in schools for children who belong to the LGBTQ community.

11

Harry Truman to Harry Styles

Harry S. Truman was the thirty-third President of the United States, considered to be one of the best presidents in US history. He ranks as fifth best in the polls behind Lincoln, Franklin D. Roosevelt, Washington, and Theodore Roosevelt. Truman was the running mate of Franklin D. Roosevelt and took over the presidency after only three months in 1945, following Roosevelt's death.

Harry Styles was never a US President (you have to be thirty-five to even run) and it's probably safe to say he never will be. However, his boyishly handsome good looks and his musical talents landed him a spot in the boy band One Direction. The band's debut song "What Makes You Beautiful" has sold over five million copies worldwide, making it among one of the best-selling singles of all time.

These men may be tough guys on the outside, but it's no secret these two are both **momma's boys**. Pretty cute, right? Truman was very close to his mother, who was exceedingly supportive of him, particularly during his childhood. She encouraged his interests in music, reading, and history. As president, he asked for political as well as personal advice from her.

Styles is known for his close relationship with his mother as well. When asked which of Styles's accomplishments he is most proud of, he says it's the things his mother considers the most impressive. His mother has revealed that her son will call her up to five times a day, unless there's a massive time difference between them, in which case he texts that he loves and misses her.

Styles isn't the only one with musical talent! Both Truman and Styles are **musicians**. Turns out, they both can **play the piano**. Truman had bad eyesight his whole life, creating barriers for him to overcome. He wasn't able to participate in sports as a child, so he turned to music. He got up at five every morning to practice the piano, which he studied twice a week until he was fifteen and continued playing into adulthood. Styles, being a member of a band, decided about three years ago that he wanted to learn to play the piano because he's eager to discover other artistic endeavors. He's got the voice, but he wanted to be able to play an instrument, too. He has taken many regular lessons with a tutor to improve his piano skills.

These two successful dudes didn't use education to move up in the world. In fact, they **didn't earn a college**

degree. Truman had dreams of attending West Point, but he was refused an appointment because of his poor eyesight. Following his high school graduation in 1901, Truman worked at a variety of jobs. He found employment in farming, oil drilling, and banking before enlisting in the army during World War I in 1917. He then ran for the county judge position in his state of Missouri, then for the US Senate, and finally as Roosevelt's running mate. He is the most recent president to not earn a college degree.

Styles attended Holmes Chapel Comprehensive School in England and took his GCSEs (final high school exams in the UK) before auditioning as a solo singer on *The X Factor* in 2010. Failing to progress in the show being a solo act, he was matched up with four other solo boys his age to make a group. That's when the magic happened. Styles thought of the name One Direction, and they came in third place on *The X Factor* that year. Simon Cowell signed them to his record label, and the rest is history.

These Harrys are also both **Democrats**. Well, sort of. As a teenager, Harry Truman worked as a page at the 1900 Democratic National Convention, and his father had many friends who were active in the Democratic Party, helping Truman gain his first political position. He gained the vice presidential nomination in 1944 to join Roosevelt. Harry Styles's political views are linked to the Labour Party of the

UK, which is a center-left political party. In the UK, instead of the Democratic Party and Republican Party, they have the Labour Party and the Conservative Party. The Labour Party contains trends that are socially democratic.

Truman and Styles have both had the honor of **meeting the queen of England**. Right before her coronation, Harry Truman met then Princess Elizabeth when she came to Washington D.C. in 1951. She and Prince Philip stayed with Truman and his family at Blair House because the White House was undergoing major renovations. Princess Elizabeth delighted Truman and the American people. Truman told Elizabeth that, according to his wife, "Whenever anyone becomes acquainted with you they immediately fall in love." How charming. Harry Styles met Queen Elizabeth in 2012 along with the other One Direction boys during the Royal Variety Performance in London, England. Styles was star struck and wrote on Twitter that night, "Today, I met the queen. Amazing night. Can't believe it!"

12

Jack Kerouac to Jack Nicholson

Jack Kerouac is an American novelist and poet, considered one of the greatest writers in American history. His most famous novels are *On the Road*, *The Town and the City*, and *Big Sur*. He's an author known for spontaneous expression in his work and for covering a variety of topics, from Catholicism to jazz to Buddhism to drugs. During his time, he became an underground celebrity and is considered a parent of the hippie movement. Kerouac continues to be part of American culture, being depicted in two films and having his novels *On the Road* and *Big Sur* turned into films, all in the past decade.

Jack Nicholson is a well-known American actor and filmmaker, known for his quirky roles as dark, neurotic characters. He has starred in classic films such as *One Flew Over the Cuckoo's Nest*, *The Shining*, *A Few Good Men*, and *As Good as It Gets*. Nicholson has been nominated for twelve Academy Awards during his career, making him the most nominated male actor in Academy history.

Jack Kerouac and Jack Nicholson were both **raised in the Catholic religion**. Kerouac was deeply close with his mother, who was a devout Catholic. He adopted her faith and stayed religious his entire life. Kerouac's *On the Road*, based on events from his own life, is about two Catholic friends searching for God. Kerouac is actually known as an American Catholic author, and his diary revealed his dedication to his religion, with every page showing some sort of religious symbol or prayer, often asking Christ to be forgiven. Kerouac also studied Buddhism during his lifetime.

Jack Nicholson was raised Catholic by his mother as well. Unlike Kerouac, he didn't continue to practice the religion and became inactive in the church during high school. He now considers himself nonreligious though he doesn't identify as an atheist and has explored other belief systems. Nicholson has been quoted hilariously saying he only prays when he goes jogging.

Kerouac and Nicholson both have **Irish roots**. Kerouac was born in Lowell, Massachusetts to French Canadian parents. However, his last name can be traced to Irish roots. In multiple interviews, Kerouac has stated that his ancestors may have come from Ireland and that his last name is an Irish word for "language of the water." Nicholson was born in Neptune City, New Jersey, to a mother of Irish descent. His grandparents, who he believed were his real parents until later in life, raised him.

Both of these men are associated with a **posse** within their own industries. Kerouac is associated with the Beat Generation that includes other writers such as Allen Ginsberg, Neal Cassady, John Clellon Holmes, Herbert Huncke, and William S. Burroughs. He met these men in his early adulthood and would be inspired by them from then on. It is believed that these men formed the basis of characters in Kerouac's own novels. Nicholson lived next door to actor Marlon Brando and near actor Warren Beatty, which led to their street being nicknamed "Bad Boy Drive." After Brando's death, Nicholson bought his bungalow for $6.1 million and tore it down out of respect for his friend.

These men have both encountered run-ins with **memory loss**. Kerouac joined the United States Merchant Marine in 1942 and then the United States Navy in 1943. However, Kerouac only served eight days on duty before being put on the sick list. Kerouac had gone to the doctor to ask for aspirin for his headaches, and the doctor ended up diagnosing him with dementia praecox, which causes trouble with mental functioning in attention and memory. After being diagnosed as having a "schizoid personality," Kerouac was honorably discharged on the grounds of psychiatric needs.

In 2013, rumors spread around that Nicholson was retiring from acting due to memory loss. The rumors stated he was having trouble remembering the lines in his scripts, but later, an unidentified source informed *NBC News* that Nicholson was still actively reading scripts and wasn't retiring.

Though they both decided to pursue careers in other fields, Kerouac and Nicholson can both be considered **artists**. Kerouac loved to paint and often turned to art when expressing his religious devotions. He did not like his title as "the king of the beat generation" and didn't want to be considered a beatnik. He once showed a reporter his painting of Pope Paul VI as proof that he wasn't a beatnik but really just a Catholic man.

Nicholson's grandmother, whom he was raised by, was an amateur artist. She seemed to have passed along her artistic abilities to Nicholson, who excelled in art as well. When Nicholson first came to Hollywood, he worked as a simple gofer for animation legends William Hanna and Joseph Barbera, creators of *The Flintstones*, *The Jetsons*, *Scooby-Doo*, and *Tom and Jerry* at MGM cartoon studio. These legends saw Nicholson's talent as an artist and offered him a starting-level position as an animation artist. Nicholson, however, declined the offer and stated his dreams were to be an actor and not an artist.

13

James Taylor to Taylor Swift

James Taylor is an American folk rock singer–songwriter and guitarist. He is known best for his famous songs "Fire and Rain," "Something in the Way She Moves," "Carolina in My Mind," and his recording of "You've Got a Friend." After Taylor came out with his breakout song, "Fire and Rain," in 1970, he became and has remained one of the most recognized and well-liked artists in the industry.

Taylor Swift is an American country-turned-pop singer–songwriter, known for her narrative songs describing personal experiences. She is one of the best-selling artists of all time and the youngest person to make it on *Forbes* magazine's "100 Most Powerful Women" list. She is a megastar in the music industry, owns four Guinness World Records, and is the first artist since The Beatles to stay six or more weeks at number one with three consecutive studio albums.

Turns out, Taylor Swift was **named** after James Taylor. Swift's parents were fans of James Taylor, and Swift's mother thought giving their daughter a gender-neutral name would help her make a business career for herself. Swift's parents introduced her to James Taylor's music at a young age, and he turned into one of Swift's largest role models.

Swift and Taylor both got their start in the music business at a young age. In fact, they both **noticed their talent and enjoyment of music at age fourteen**. James Taylor wrote his first song on guitar at age fourteen and started a band with his friend Danny Kortchmar, who immediately recognized Taylor's talent.

When Swift was twelve, she learned how to play three chords on a guitar and wrote her first song, "Lucky You." As an eighth grader, Swift made an artist development deal and traveled to Nashville multiple times. When Swift was fourteen, her family moved to Nashville to help her pursue her dreams of being a country music star.

These talented artists **moved from their hometowns as teens to pursue a music career**. James Taylor checked into McLean Hospital in Belmont, Massachusetts during his senior year of high school for his depression. Taylor was grateful for the time he spent there making strides toward being mentally healthy. He finished out his schooling in the hospital, and after graduating at age eighteen, he checked out of McLean and headed to New York City. His friend Kortchmar convinced him it was the place to form a band. They called themselves The Flying Machine, and they only lasted a year before the band broke up and Taylor went solo. Turns out that was a good move.

At age fourteen, Swift moved to Nashville, Tennessee to get serious about making it in the music business. Her parents were huge supporters. Swift says of her parents, "They knew nothing about the industry and had no involvement in entertainment, but I was obsessed with it, and so they did their research and read up about it to help me in every way they could. They're amazing people." Her big move from her home in Pennsylvania to Tennessee paid off, and Swift got signed to a record deal that same year.

Speaking of record deals, James Taylor and Taylor Swift both **completed firsts when signing at their record companies**. James Taylor, at age nineteen, was connected to Peter Asher, the head of The Beatles' new record label, Apple Records. Asher showed Paul McCartney some of Taylor's music, and McCartney immediately noticed his greatness. Taylor became the first non-British act signed to Apple Records.

Taylor Swift, at age fourteen, was signed to Sony/ATV Tree publishing house. Swift was the youngest songwriter ever signed by the company. However, Swift left the Sony/ATV Tree at age fifteen, unhappy with the company wanting her to only record other artists' songs until she was eighteen and ready to release her own album. Swift felt she was already ready to do so, and a year later, she signed with the new independent record label, Big Machine Records. Swift was one of the very first artists to be signed with the company. At age sixteen, she immediately started writing her debut album, *Taylor Swift*, released a year later.

These musicians might have very different styles and audiences, as well as a large age difference, but they both **fought for the number one *Billboard* spot in 2015**. James Taylor's *Mud Slide Slim and the Blue Horizon*, his 1971 album, reached number two in the album charts and was his most popular album. That's until 2015, when he released *Before This World*, and it skyrocketed to the top. *Before This World* replaced Swift's *1989* at the number one *Billboard* spot.

Talent is something neither of these artists lacks. They each lay claim to **many Grammy Awards**. James Taylor is a five-time Grammy winner, was inducted into the Songwriters Hall of Fame in 2000, and was named Person of the Year by Grammy Award-sponsored MusiCares. Taylor Swift is a seven-time Grammy winner, was honored by the Songwriters Hall of Fame in 2010, and is the only woman ever named twice for *Billboard*'s Woman of the Year.

Taylor Swift listened to James Taylor growing up and admired his music greatly. He quickly became one of her idols. With Swift's rise in fame, she reached out to James Taylor to perform with her. James Taylor and Taylor Swift have **performed together** on two separate occasions, once in 2011 during Swift's Speak Now World Tour and once in 2012 when Swift appeared as Taylor's special guest during a concert at Tanglewood. James Taylor said of Swift, "She and I worked together, and we just hit it off. I loved her songs, and her presence on stage was so great. She told me that her mom had me in mind when she named her Taylor. When she called and asked if I would join her at the end of the last tour to celebrate the end of a successful tour on her part, I jumped in."

14

JANE AUSTEN TO JANE GOODALL

Jane Austen was an English novelist whose famous works of romantic fiction led her to become one of the most widely read writers in all of English literature. She is one of the most famous female writers in history. Her historical importance comes from her special style of humor, realism, irony, and social commentary in her writing. Some of her famous works include *Pride and Prejudice*, *Sense and Sensibility*, *Emma*, and *Mansfield Park*. Many of her books have been adapted into films and are still taught in classrooms all over the world.

Jane Goodall is that really cool primatologist who studies the behavior of chimpanzees. She's considered to be the world's leading expert on chimpanzees and is the founder of the Jane Goodall Institute for the conservation and welfare of animals. She is known for her fifty-five-year study of social and family behaviors of wild chimpanzees in Tanzania.

They've each had a worldwide impact for their work and are well-known figures in America, but these women are actually both **English**. Jane Austen was born in Hampshire, England

and grew up with six brothers and one sister. Throughout her life, she lived with her immediate family in multiple places in England. Jane Goodall was born in London, England with one sister. Her father gave her a lifelike chimpanzee toy, which started her love of animals. Today, Goodall still has the toy, and it sits on her dresser in London. So cute!

These two women are considered extremely successful and brilliant people, but they actually had **little schooling**. Jane Austen was sent to Oxford along with her sister and closest friend Cassandra, but soon after, both girls caught typhus, and Jane even came close to dying. Good thing she fought through it! Can you imagine a world without *Pride and Prejudice*? I can't! Austen was then homeschooled and eventually attended boarding school but wasn't able to finish because her family couldn't afford it. The remainder of Austen's education was simply reading books and learning from her father and two of her brothers. Austen's love of writing was encouraged, and as a child, she would write short poems, stories, and plays just for her family's enjoyment.

Jane Goodall did not earn a BA from college but instead leapt right into a PhD from Cambridge University. Even though she had no degree, she was only the eighth person ever allowed to study there without previously earning a BA. She was tutored by a zoologist professor and completed a thesis entitled "Behaviour of the Free-Ranging Chimpanzee."

Austen and Goodall both **started their successful careers at age twenty-three**. By the time Jane Austen was twenty-three, she had completely finished her first two full-length novels, *Sense and Sensibility* and *Pride and Prejudice*. Austen read these novels to her family aloud, just as she had done when she was a child. Her family praised her for *Pride and Prejudice*, telling her it was their favorite of her works so far. It was at this point that Austen's father wrote to publishers asking if they would consider publishing his daughter's work. However, it wasn't until she was thirty-six that a publisher agreed to publish her books and would only do so if her name were kept anonymous.

At age twenty-two, Jane Goodall had moved to Africa to follow her passion of animals. She worked as a secretary for her friend until reaching out to Kenyan archaeologist Louis Leaky who then hired Goodall at age twenty-three. He sent her to study primate behavior in London and then to Tanzania, where she performed her famous study.

Jane Austen gained her fame by being an exceptional writer, but these women are actually both **authors**. Jane Goodall is actually the author of twenty-six books documenting her knowledge of chimpanzees and her life spent studying them. Eight of her books are geared toward children and display facts and photos about chimpanzees as well as adorable fiction stories about animals. Her most recent book was published in 2013, at the age of seventy-nine, where Goodall discusses the critical importance of trees and plants as well as steps one can take to protect the nature around us.

15

Joan of Arc to Joan Jett

Joan of Arc is considered to be a major heroine of France for leading the French army. She is also a Roman Catholic saint. She claims to have experienced visions with instructions from Archangel Michael, Saint Margaret, and Saint Catherine to save France in the Hundred Years' War. The King of France at the time, Charles VII, sent this brave, illiterate farm girl to lead the siege of Orléans as part of a relief mission. The battle ended up being a turning point in the war and Joan of Arc's first major military victory. After additional victories, she was captured and handed over to the English, who put her on trial for a variety of charges. She was found guilty and was burned at the stake at age nineteen. Joan Jett, also known as the Godmother of Punk, is an American Rock guitarist, singer, and songwriter of the band Joan Jett & the Blackhearts. They produced the record *I Love Rock 'n Roll*, which reached number one on the *Billboard* Hot 100 chart. Other popular songs recorded by the band include "Crimson and Clover," "I Hate Myself for Loving You," and "Bad Reputation." Her first band, the Runaways, produced the hit song "Cherry Bomb." In 2015, she was inducted into the Rock and Roll Hall of Fame.

Joan of Arc and Joan Jett both **found their calling at age seventeen**. After gaining the support of two soldiers at age seventeen, Joan of Arc met with the military commander Robert de Baudricourt to ask for permission to visit the royal French court. She remarked about a military reversal in the war several days before messengers arrived to report on it. Baudricourt considered the distance of the battle's location and felt Joan could've only known this information if she heard it by divine revelation, as she had claimed. He granted her permission to see Charles VII, whom she impressed and gained authorization from to travel with the French army. Joan Jett became the founding member of the Runaways at age seventeen in 1975. The all-female rock band went on to record and produce music until breaking up in 1979. Joan Jett continued with a solo career until forming the band Joan Jett & the Blackhearts.

Clearly, we aren't talking about girly girls. These two tough chicks wore **men's clothing**. When traveling to visit the royal French court, Joan of Arc was disguised as a male soldier as a precaution. She wore armor and protective clothing during battle as well as male clothing in prison to deter men from assaulting her. This later led to cross-dressing charges against her.

Joan Jett is known for her unapologetic hard look, consisting of leather jackets, rocker t-shirts, black jeans, and converse shoes. She's also known for being against bras and refusing to wear them. In other words, Joan Jett's look is all about being anti-feminine and very masculine.

These trailblazing women have actually both **been in jail**. Joan of Arc had her fair share of jail time. She was captured and put in prison, awaiting trial for heresy and cross-dressing. Instead of being confined in a religious prison under the supervision of women nuns, she was placed in the secular prison guarded by their own soldiers.

The first time Jett went to England with the Runaways, the band was thrown in jail for theft. The girls just wanted to keep their room keys as souvenirs, but they were stopped at the border and arrested. While in holding, the girls got their luggage searched, and band member Cherie Currie realized their road manager had stashed some of his cocaine in her makeup case. The kind guard felt sorry for the girls and pretended he didn't see it so they could move along. Can you say lucky?

It goes without saying that these two are **feminist icons**. Joan of Arc was something of a "protofeminist" in her time, carving the way for strong women to come. During the suffragette era, she was a poster girl for the Women's Movement. She appeared on posters wearing suffragette colors and calling for equality. She was an inspiration for women's right to vote in elections due to her own involvement in military strategy and having her voice heard.

Joan Jett has been considered a feminist icon throughout her career, often called the "Queen of Rock 'n Roll." Her songs are repeatedly called female empowerment anthems. Songs such as "Bad Reputation," is all about being an independent woman and not apologizing for it. She has spent her career convincing the world women can rock just as hard, and they can talk about sex, booze, and life on the streets just as much as the boys. When inducted into the Rock and Roll Hall of Fame in 2015, she used her time in the spotlight to say that there should be more women in the Hall of Fame.

16

John D. Rockefeller to Johnny Depp

John Davison Rockefeller Sr. was an American business-man and philanthropist of great influence. As the co-founder of Standard Oil Company, which dominated the US oil indus-try, his wealth skyrocketed. Rockefeller quickly became the world's richest man and the first American worth more than a billion dollars. Upon his death, his fortune was at $336 bil-lion, actually accounting for 1.5 percent of the entire national economy, making him the richest person in US history.

Johnny Depp is an American actor, producer, and musician. He has won a Golden Globe Award as well as a Screen Actors Guild Award for Best Actor. He is most famous for movies such as *Edward Scissorhands*, *Pirates of the Caribbean*, *Charlie and the Chocolate Factory*, *Alice in Wonderland*, and *Sweeny Todd*. In 2012, he was listed in the Guinness World Records book as the highest paid actor, earning $75 million.

Rockefeller and Depp both have **English ancestry**. Rockefeller was born in Richford, New York and was the second of six children. His father, con artist Bill Rockefeller, was of English and German descent. Depp was born in Owensboro, Kentucky and was the youngest of four children. Depp is mostly of English descent and has New England as well as Colonial New York roots. He's actually the twentieth cousin of Queen Elizabeth II. Interestingly, Depp is also of 3/2048 African descent and the distant relative of an African slave whose biracial daughter, Elizabeth Key Grinstead, was the first woman in North America to sue for her freedom from slavery and win.

Though they ended up being extremely successful men, Rockefeller and Depp had **humble beginnings**. Rockefeller grew up with little money and did his share of regular chores. He also earned extra money by raising turkeys and selling potatoes and candy. The little money he earned from these endeavors he lent to neighbors. After taking a ten-week business college course for bookkeeping, at age sixteen he got his first job as an assistant bookkeeper. The salary for his first three months was fifty cents a day. Yikes! He would celebrate the day he got this job, September 26, as "job day" for the rest of his life, and it was considered more important to him than his birthday.

Depp got a guitar from his mother at age twelve and started playing in garage bands, dropping out of high school at age seventeen to become a rock musician. He regretted this decision and tried to go back to school two weeks later, but his principle told him to continue following his dreams instead. His band, The Kids, traveled to Los Angeles to get a record deal, but the band split up before doing so. Depp married his first wife, his bass player's sister, and worked odd jobs including being a telemarketer for pens. His wife, a makeup artist, introduced him to Nicolas Cage who advised him to pursue an acting career.

Speaking of music, these men actually both had **a love of music**. In high school, Rockefeller was a dedicated and well-behaved student. He especially excelled in debate and music, dreaming of a possible future career in the music industry. Rockefeller had a deep love of music, paralleled by Depp who also started his interest in music at a young age. In addition to forming a band, Depp has continued playing guitar throughout his lifetime. He has played guitar on an Oasis song, the soundtrack of his movie *Chocolat*, a cover of Carly Simon's "You're So Vain," and live with Marilyn Manson. He has also appeared in a number of artists' music videos, including those of Tom Petty, Avril Lavigne, and Paul McCartney.

Rockefeller and Depp didn't keep all of their profits to themselves. They are both **philanthropists**, giving great deals of money to charities and good causes. Rockefeller is particularly known for his philanthropy, giving in total around $550 million. As a devout Baptist, he gave one tenth of his annual earnings to his church. Rockefeller was also an abolitionist and gave major funds to a college in Atlanta for African American women, which became Spelman College, named after Rockefeller's wife, Cettie Spelman. The University of Chicago was founded due to a great donation of $80 million by Rockefeller, and he created the General Education Board to promote education in all parts of the country. Rockefeller became one of the first great benefactors of medical science, with contributions that led to the development of a yellow fever vaccine and the complete eradication of hookworm disease. He also created the Rockefeller Foundation, which focused on public health, medical training, and the arts.

Depp's contributions to charity hit close to home. His daughter, Lily-Rose Melody Depp, recovered from a serious illness in 2007, caused by an E. coli infection that began to cause her kidneys to shut down. She stayed in Great Ormond Street Hospital for an extended period of time. Depp, to thank the hospital for taking care of his daughter, dressed as his famous character, Captain Jack Sparrow, and spent four hours reading stories to the sick children at the hospital. He also gave $2 million to the hospital. Depp has contributed to a book, Celebrity Handprints, raising money for children's charities. He has even been awarded a Courage to Care Award for his longtime advocacy of children and children's charities.

When times got tough, you can bet these two men wouldn't turn to drinking. Both Rockefeller and Depp **quit drinking**. Rockefeller submitted to total abstinence from alcohol and tobacco throughout his life, probably due to his religious beliefs. He passed this example down to his son, John D. Rockefeller Jr., who contributed to the founding of Alcoholics Anonymous to assist recovering alcoholics.

Depp, though he drank alcohol for a large part of his life, revealed at age fifty that he consciously quit drinking. Deciding he had already gotten everything he could get out of it, Depp broke it off with alcohol because he just doesn't have the physical need for it and can function fine without it.

17

Leonardo da Vinci to Leonardo DiCaprio

Leonardo da Vinci was an Italian man of many talents and is considered to be one of the smartest people to ever live. He is known for his skills in painting, including, of course, works like the *Mona Lisa* and *The Last Supper*. Other than being a painter, da Vinci was also a sculptor, architect, musician, mathematician, engineer, inventor, anatomist, geologist, cartographer, botanist, and writer. Wow, that's a lot of talents! He is also referred to as "the Father of paleontology."

However impressive he is, he wasn't ever an actor or film producer like our American treasure Leonardo DiCaprio. You might know this Leonardo from *The Titanic*, *Catch Me If You Can*, *Shutter Island*, *Inception*, *The Great Gatsby*, or *The Wolf of Wall Street*. He has won two Golden Globe Awards and five Academy Awards.

An obvious comparison is that these two have the same **name**, but it is also true that this was intentionally done. When DiCaprio's mom was pregnant with him, she and DiCaprio's dad happened to be in a gallery in Florence, Italy. They were looking at some of the great works of da Vinci. When looking at one of the paintings done by the famous artist, DiCaprio kicked for the first time. According to DiCaprio, his father took this as a cosmic sign, and the couple decided his name had to be Leonardo.

From the name Leonardo, it's easy to assume these two men are **Italian**. Leonardo da Vinci was born in Vinci in the region of Tuscany, Italy, and spent most of his childhood there. Both of his parents were also Italian. Once his professional career started, he lived in other places around Italy and, for a period, spent some time living in France. Leonardo DiCaprio has Italian roots from his father who is half Italian and came from the Naples area in Italy.

Leonardo da Vinci and DiCaprio were both **raised Roman Catholic**. Leonardo da Vinci was baptized into the Roman Catholic Church, but because of his in-depth research and dedication to science, he had a hard time relying on the faith-based teachings of Christianity. He was far from being a devout Catholic, writing very little about religion, and created religious paintings simply because he was commissioned to do so. Leonardo DiCaprio shares this stray from Catholic roots by claiming he is non-religious, but he isn't an atheist. In other words, da Vinci and DiCaprio seem relatively uninterested in religion.

Another thing they have in common is that they were both an **only child**. Leonardo da Vinci was actually the result of an out-of-wedlock relationship between his father, a wealthy Florentine legal notary named Piero da Vinci, and a peasant named Caterina. He was the only child of his wealthy father and peasant mother, until he gained a few half siblings from is father's third and forth marriages when Leonardo was in his twenties. Leonardo DiCaprio was the only child born from parents Irmelin and George DiCaprio. When Leonardo was one year old, his parents split up, and he remained an only child.

Speaking of parents, both da Vinci and DiCaprio were **raised by their mother**. Though there is little known about Leonardo da Vinci's childhood, we know he spent at least the first five years of his life on a small settlement within a village in Vinci with his peasant mother. She took care of him until he was moved to his father's home when he was a little older. Leonardo DiCaprio lived mostly with his mother after his parent's divorce. He and his mother lived in several different neighborhoods in the LA area. His mother worked several jobs to support them both.

Leonardo da Vinci and Leonardo DiCaprio surprisingly both struggled with a **mental or learning disorder** during their lifetimes. Da Vinci struggled with dyslexia, a learning disorder which leads to difficulty with reading despite normal intelligence. Problems include not being able to sound out words, read quickly, write words, pronounce words, or understand what was read.

DiCaprio revealed to Katy Couric in 2004 that he struggled with obsessive-compulsive disorder (OCD) for most of his adult life. OCD is a mental disorder that occurs when excessive thoughts lead to repetitive behaviors. He often feels the need to walk through doorways multiple times.

Both have a **connection to the LGBT community**. It is heavily speculated that da Vinci was gay, and famous psychologist Sigmund Freud also supports this. In a letter from Freud to a mother of a gay son who wished him to be "treated" by Freud, the psychoanalysis expert comforted her by telling her that being gay is neither a crime nor a sickness. In the letter he states, "Many highly respectable individuals of ancient and modern times have been homosexuals, several of the greatest men among them." He then lists the names of Plato, Michelangelo, and Leonardo da Vinci as examples.

DiCaprio himself isn't gay, but he is a gay rights activist. He donated $61,000 to the Gay & Lesbian Alliance Against Defamation (GLAAD) in 2013, an organization dedicated to promoting the image of the LGBT community in the media.

18

Marilyn Monroe to Meryl Streep

Marilyn Monroe and Meryl Streep are easily two of the most celebrated and recognizable actresses. Marilyn is a dynamite sex symbol who transformed the world of celebrity. She starred in many major movies of her time, such as *Gentlemen Prefer Blondes*, *The Seven Year Itch*, and *Some Like It Hot*.

Meryl Streep, though not considered a sex symbol by any means, shares Marilyn's signature blonde hair, bright blue eyes, and translucent pale skin. Meryl Streep is considered one of the greatest film actors of all time and has received three Academy Awards. She is known for her ability to perfect different accents. She has appeared in movies such as *The Devil Wears Prada*, *Mamma Mia!*, *The Iron Lady*, and *Into the Woods*.

Starting from the very beginning, both of these blonde beauties were **born with a different name**. Marilyn Monroe was first named Norma Jeane Mortensen. Not a very attractive name, now is it? At age twenty, Marilyn gained a contract deal with 20th Century Fox, and the executive, Ben Lyon, told her she needed a stage name. After deciding to adopt her mother's maiden name of Monroe, she debated between Norma Monroe or Jeane Monroe. Lyon told her that these names were too common, instead suggesting Marilyn because she reminded him of Marilyn Miller.

Meryl Streep was born with the name Mary Louise Streep, after her mother, whose name was also Mary. She combined her first and middle name to be Meryl, a more unique and recognizable name.

These leading ladies also have their choices of living location in common. Marilyn and Meryl both **lived in NYC and LA**. Marilyn was born in Los Angeles in 1926 but moved around to various foster homes around the state of California after her mother, Gladys, gave her up. She became a resident of New York during her breakthrough period in 1955. Marilyn lived in forty-three different homes in her lifetime but only owned one. This home is in Brentwood, Los Angeles and is the home where she was sadly found dead at age thirty-six.

Meryl grew up in New Jersey but moved to New York in 1975 at the age of twenty-six. New York is where she made her debut as an actress. After getting married to her current husband and having four children, Meryl moved into a $3 million mansion in Los Angeles.

Speaking of Los Angeles, Marilyn and Meryl both have their very own **Hollywood Walk of Fame stars** on Hollywood Boulevard. Marilyn earned hers in 1960, and it is located on the popular 6700 block in front of McDonalds. Meryl earned hers in 1998, and hers is located in the most coveted placement of all, in front of the Roosevelt Hotel.

In addition to both being actresses, Marilyn and Meryl have both acted in **dramas, comedies, and musicals**. Though Marilyn acted mostly in the comedy genre, 45 comedies in total, she also acted in 7 musicals and 34 dramas. In 1954, Marilyn played Vicky Parker in *There's No Business Like Show Business*, which is actually a drama, comedy, and musical all in one. Meryl has even appeared in the documentary genre, with an astounding total of 139, as well as 82 comedies and 12 musicals. Meryl is well known for her role as Donna in *Mamma Mia!*, classified as both a musical and a comedy.

Since both are recognized actresses, it is natural that they both have received **multiple Golden Globes**. Marilyn has won three Golden Globes, including Best Actress for *Some Like It Hot*, and she was nominated for one other. Meryl has won eight Golden Globes and was nominated for twenty more. Her most recent win was in 2012 for Best Actress for her film *The Iron Lady*.

Like most Hollywood stars, Marilyn and Meryl are both **Democrats**. Marilyn was reportedly registered as a Democrat and lived her whole life as a liberal Democrat. Meryl is also a Democrat, making contributions to Obama's campaign in 2008. In fact, all of her other contributions, totaling $30,000 since 1981, have been to Democrats. She is humble about her religious and political views but takes an active role in good causes. Her most recent involvement with the government was when she urged Congress to build a National Women's History Museum in Washington D.C., arguing for the importance of giving great women recognition on the National Mall.

19

MARK TWAIN TO MARK WAHLBERG

Mark Twain is easily one of the most famous writers to ever walk the planet. His novel *Adventures of Huckleberry Finn* is called "The Great American Novel." He is also known for his witty sense of humor in both his writing and speech. Twain was a friend to presidents, artists, industrialists, and European royalty. He had a very close friendship with Nikola Tesla, completely fascinated by science and discovery.

Mark Wahlberg is the bad boy of the Hollywood industry, a rapper turned model turned actor and producer. He has starred in multiple successful films, including *Planet of the Apes*, *The Departed*, *The Other Guys*, *The Fighter* (which earned him an Academy Award for Best Picture nomination), *Ted*, and *Lone Survivor*. He also produced the popular HBO series *Entourage*, which he based on his life in Hollywood.

These two big-shots were part of **big families**. Mark Twain, born Samuel Langhorne Clemens, was the sixth of seven children. His family lived in a small house in Missouri and only three of his siblings survived childhood. By the time Twain was six, he had already lost three of his siblings.

Mark Wahlberg was the youngest of nine children. He grew up in Boston, Massachusetts, and soon began a life of crime. With four of his siblings in and out of jail, Wahlberg was following the example he was given. He has since taken full responsibility for his crimes and said his upbringing wasn't to blame. According to him, he knew right from wrong and chose the wrong path anyway.

In addition to coming from big families, Twain and Wahlberg are both of **English and Irish descent**. Twain has ancestors of Scots-Irish and English descent. Wahlberg's father is of Irish descent and so is his mother, who is also of English descent. Through his mother, Wahlberg is actually related to great American novelist Nathaniel Hawthorne, best known for writing *The Scarlet Letter*. Looks like Twain and Wahlberg's families both had some great writers!

Though they ended up extremely successful, these two were **school dropouts**. When Mark Twain was eleven, his father passed. The next school year, following the fifth grade, Twain decided not to attend. Instead, he became a printer's apprentice where he worked as a typesetter and contributed to the *Hannibal Journal*, a newspaper his older brother owned. Twain also educated himself by spending time at public libraries, where there was a greater depth of knowledge available to him. At age eighteen, Twain left his brother's newspaper and set out for New York to work as a printer. He married at age thirty-five, became a journalist, and started writing his great novels a few years after.

Mark Wahlberg attended Copley Square High School in Boston but never graduated. As a youth, Wahlberg was in trouble twenty to twenty-five times with the Boston Police Department and came into fame after being an original member of the boy band New Kids on the Block, of which his older brother Donnie was also a member. He only stayed in the band three months before quitting, and he began recording with other rappers, with whom he formed the band Marky Mark and the Funky Bunch. With the famous Calvin Klein underwear shoot, Wahlberg gained fame and got involved in the acting business.

Both of these men owe at least some of their fame to being **humorists**. Twain is a humor writer, and Wahlberg is a humor performer. Twain started out writing light, humorous pieces, but his wit and satire mixed with solid narrative gained him fame with his novels *The Adventures of Tom Sawyer* and *Adventures of Huckleberry Finn.* The Mark Twain Prize for American Humor is America's premier award for humor and has been given by the John F. Kennedy Center for the Performing Arts since 1998. Winners of this award include famous comedians such as Steve Martin, Ellen DeGeneres, Will Ferrell, Tina Fey, and Eddie Murphy.

Though Wahlberg is not considered a comedian, he has acted in and produced multiple comedy films and TV series. One of his most successful comedies, *Ted*, was Universal's highest-grossing film in 2012. *The Other Guys*, in which he starred alongside Will Ferrell, was a box office success and grossed over $170 million. His HBO series, *Entourage,* was the winner of six Primetime Emmy Awards for the acting, directing, writing, and Outstanding Comedy Series catego- ries. The series was turned into a feature film and debuted in 2015.

Twain and Wahlberg were born and raised **Christian**. Mark Twain identified as a Presbyterian and participated in religious discussions. He attended services, especially to deal with the deaths of those he loved and the prospect of his own mortality. Twain thought critically about religion and expressed his doubt in the goodness of God, who was supposed to be all-powerful for good or evil, yet let evil things happen on Earth. He contemplated whether God created the world with tortures for his own purpose and was indifferent toward humanity and its insignificance.

Mark Wahlberg is a committed Roman Catholic, asserting that he starts his day by praying, and after leaving his house every morning, he stops at the church to thank God before continuing with his day. Though he is a religious person and admits to being impressed by the Catholic Church's Pope Francis, he doesn't agree with the church's view on gay marriage, something he supports.

These two men at one point in their lives have made racist comments but since have **changed their views on people of other races**. Mark Twain was always a dedicated supporter of the abolitionist movement to end slavery and praised Lincoln's Proclamation, saying it "not only set the black slaves free, but set the white man free also." He felt that America was not fair to those who were non-white, stating that the Chinese were also mistreated and abused. However, as sensitive as he was to race politics, he made some offensive claims about Native Americans in his early writings, calling them "the scum of the earth." He later made an argument against his own statements, recognizing how these people had also been mistreated, and detested how white men called them "savages." Mark Wahlberg had his own run-in with hate speech as a young boy when, on two separate occasions at age fifteen, he harassed African American children by throwing rocks and yelling racial slurs. At age sixteen, he assaulted a Vietnamese man on the street using a long wooden stick and yelling racial slurs at him as well. For these crimes, he was charged with attempted murder and served time. He has since apologized and asked forgiveness after reconnecting with the Catholic faith.

Twain and Wahlberg didn't just grow up with similar family size, they also had similar families as adults. Both Marks had **one wife and four children**. Twain, when living in Buffalo, New York with his wife, had one son and three daughters: Langdon, Susy, Clara, and Jean. Wahlberg lives with his family in Beverly Hills. He and his wife have two sons and two daughters. Of his daughters, Wahlberg says, "Having two daughters changed my perspective on a lot of things, and I definitely have a newfound respect for women. And I think I finally became a good and real man when I had a daughter." How sweet!

20

MARTIN LUTHER KING JR. TO MARTIN SCORSESE

Martin Luther King Jr. was the amazing American Baptist minister and activist who famously lead the African-American Civil Rights Movement. He was known for his nonviolent civil disobedience tactics and his disapproval of violence. He led many memorable protests including the Montgomery Bus Boycott of 1955, the March on Washington in 1963 where he delivered the amazing "I Have a Dream" speech, and the Selma to Montgomery Marches in 1965. He was the first president of the Southern Christian Leadership Conference (SCLC), which he helped found. He received the Nobel Peace Prize in 1964 for fighting racial inequality. While planning a large occupation in Washington D.C., Dr. King was assassinated in 1968 at the young age of thirty-nine. His death caused riots and heartbreak across the nation.

Martin Scorsese is a prestigious American director, producer, and screenwriter. He's known for his films *Taxi Driver*, *Raging Bull*, *Goodfellas*, *Gangs of New York*, and *The Departed*. As one of the most significant and influential filmmakers in history, his actors have seventy total nominations for Academy Awards, BAFTA Awards, and Golden Globe Awards.

Both were **deeply religious** men. Dr. King was a Baptist preacher like his father before him. As a Christian minister, he heavily believed in the commandment of loving your neighbor as yourself, especially loving your enemies and praying for them. His peaceful protests stemmed from Jesus's teaching of nonviolence. Martin Scorsese grew up in a deeply religious Italian Catholic family, and when he was in high school, he wanted to become a Catholic priest. This is an ironic fact since priests are not allowed to marry, and he was married five times! Scorsese once said, "I am a lapsed Catholic. But, I am a Roman Catholic, and there is no getting out of it." Many of his movies reflect religious themes. One of his most personal and famous movies was *The Last Temptation of Christ*.

MLK and Scorsese also suffered with bouts of **depression** during their lifetime. Though he was a powerful, fearless leader, Dr. King secretly suffered from depression. He suffered from depression throughout most of his life. Even at age twelve, young Martin was suffering and blamed himself for his grandmother's death. He jumped out of their second story window but, thankfully, survived. This was one of two suicide attempts made by King as a child. Later in life, some of

King's staff advised him to get psychiatric treatment, but he refused. Some think King's radical empathy for his enemies came from his depression, which studies show enhance empathy toward others. In 1977, bad reviews and disappointing reception of Scorsese's film *New York, New York* drove him into a depression. During this time, he was also fighting a cocaine addiction. Even though him and star of the musical, Liza Minnelli, were both married at the time, it's rumored that they carried on an open affair during production. They broke up around the same time of the poor reception of *New York, New York*. Scorsese required hospitalization for his depression and drug abuse.

Martin Scorsese and Martin Luther King Jr. both **won multiple awards**, including recognition from *Time* magazine. Martin Luther King Jr. was *Time*'s "Man of the Year" in 2000, and Scorsese was named in *Time*'s 2007 list of the "World's 100 Most Influential People."

Though neither has been super vocal about their political views, Dr. King and Scorsese are **Democrats**. Dr. King didn't advertise his views but later admitted that he had always voted for the Democratic ticket. He privately voted for John F. Kennedy and said though he didn't publically support him during his first election, he would have supported him if President Kennedy had lived for the next election. Martin Scorsese is a loyal supporter of the Democratic Party and was a known supporter of Barack Obama during his 2008 presidential campaign.

Both **believed visual images could influence people**. Dr. King wanted the world to see the hateful prejudice shown on their local and national news so that the American public could recognize how wrong the violence was against non-violent protestors. The Bloody Sunday events of the Selma to Montgomery marches were televised, and Americans all over the country could see images of the brutal attacks on peaceful protestors, who were left bloody and injured. King was right; the images raised support for the Selma Voting Rights Campaign. Many supporters came to fight for African American rights alongside King in Selma after watching the injustice on TV.

Martin Scorsese was recently quoted as saying that our schools need to "stress visual literacy" using "moving images that engage their humanity and their intelligence." Scorsese recognizes the fact that there are visual learners in schools and that kids today resonate with visual images when learning.

21

MICHAEL JACKSON TO MICHAEL BUBLÉ

Michael Jackson is the "King of Pop" and his album *Thriller* is the best-selling album of all time, with over fifty million copies sold worldwide. Jackson has won hundreds and hundreds of awards, making him the most awarded recording artist in history. He is in the Rock and Roll Hall of Fame, Songwriters Hall of Fame, and the Dance Hall of Fame. As the *The New York Times* describes him, "In the world of pop music, there is Michael Jackson and there is everybody else." In other words, he's a big deal.

Michael Bublé is a Canadian singer who has made a name for himself in the music industry. His 2007 album, *Call Me Irresponsible*, made it to the number one spot in the UK, Canada, the US, and on several European charts. His voice and persona have repeatedly been compared to Frank Sinatra, and he remains one of the most well-liked singers in the industry with fans of all ages. Bublé has been quoted saying that Michael Jackson was the singer who had the biggest impact on him growing up.

Jackson and Bublé don't just have singing in common; they were actually both **raised Christian**. Jackson was raised as a Jehovah's Witness, a Christian denomination. As a young boy, Jackson was required to do missionary work and went from door to door distributing the Jehovah's Witness magazine, "Watchtower." Later in his life, he was excommunicated from the religion because he was becoming too "worldly," and they disapproved of his "Thriller" music video.

Bublé was raised as a Roman Catholic. When he was a teenager, Bublé admitted to sleeping with his Bible and praying to become a singer. Bublé's interest in music came as early as the age of five due to his family playing Bing Crosby's *White Christmas* album at Christmas time.

Speaking of interest in music, these two talented singers **realized their music ability at age thirteen**. When Michael Jackson was eight years old, he starting singing in The Jackson 5. Jackson was seen as a prodigy, and even though he was the youngest, he quickly became the lead singer of the group. Jackson evolved into a teen idol, and he left the Jackson 5 to start his solo career at age thirteen. He realized he could make it as a solo performer and started straying from the "bubblegum pop" music of the Jackson 5 to a more adult and complex sound.

Michael Bublé was thirteen when he and his family first realized he was a talented singer. Young Bublé was in the car with his family at Christmastime and they were singing along to "White Christmas." Apparently, he took his family by surprise when he powerfully sang the words "May your days be merry and bright." His first singing shows started at age sixteen and, he got a singing manager at age eighteen.

During their humble beginnings, the Jackson and Bublé boys were both **talent show winners**. A year after Michael Jackson joined the Jackson 5, the group won a major local talent show when they performed James Brown's "I Got You (I Feel Good)." This win gave the Jackson 5 recognition, and they started being hired to play at clubs as well as to be openers for distinguished stars such as Gladys Knight and Etta James.

When Michael Bublé was eighteen, he entered a local talent contest and won. However, he was disqualified because he was underage. Bublé took the advice of the talent show's organizer, Bev Delich, and entered the Canadian Youth Talent Search, which he also won. Delich then became Bublé's manager, and the young singer took every gig he could get, from talent shows to cruise ships to malls to bars. He was discovered performing at a business party by the Prime Minister's aide, at the time, who then introduced Bublé to the big-shot Grammy-winning producer David Foster, who had also worked with Michael Jackson.

It wasn't long into either Jackson's or Bublé's careers before they started being recognized for their excellence. These men won **multiple Grammy Awards**. Jackson received thirteen Grammy Awards as well as the Grammy Legend Award and the Grammy Lifetime Achievement Award. He received eight Grammys for just the *Thriller* album alone. Bublé was nominated for the Grammy for Best Traditional Pop Vocal Album for his first and second album, but won it for his third, forth, fifth, and sixth albums. Pretty impressive, right?

A nice similarity between these successful people is that instead of keeping all of their earnings to themselves, they both **gave numerous amounts of money to charity**. Michael Jackson is known for his contributions to the less fortunate. In fact, in 2000, *Guinness World Records* recognized Jackson as the most giving entertainer, contributing to a total of thirty-nine different charities. He was also given an award from President Ronald Reagan to commemorate Jackson's contribution to charities, helping those recovering from drug and alcohol abuse, as well as a Drunk Driving Prevention campaign. Jackson gave his entire share of the proceeds from his Victory Tour and all the profits from the single "Man in the Mirror" to charity. He even started his own charity for underprivileged children in 1992 called Heal the World. What an amazing human being.

Michael Bublé follows in Jackson's footsteps by his $50,000 contribution to those affected by the Black Saturday bushfires in Australia and by continuing to support a number of charitable projects. One of these is a children's charity called Believe in Magic, for which he took part in their Believe in Magic Wristband Fundraiser.

22

Paul Revere to Paul McCartney

Paul Revere was an American silversmith and patriot in the American Revolution. His claim to fame is the renowned "Paul Revere's Ride" in which he alerted the colonial militia to the movement of British forces before the battles of Lexington and Concord. Though he is notorious for yelling the phrase, "The British are coming!" his mission was actually one of secrecy since there were British patrollers along his ride route. In reality, he delivered his message much more stealthily and said the phrase, "The regulars are coming out."

Sir Paul McCartney, also known as "the cute Beatle," is an English singer-songwriter who gained global stardom as the bassist in the British rock band, The Beatles. Since the band's breakup in 1970, McCartney has continued as a successful solo artist. He is considered one of the greatest music composers and performers of all time with sales of one hundred million albums and one hundred million singles for his work with the Beatles and as a solo artist.

Though they later strayed from these religious views, Paul Revere and Paul McCartney were **raised in the Catholic faith**. Paul Revere was born in Boston, Massachusetts as the third of twelve children. He became interested in the Church of England, a reformed Catholic church. Revere's father was a Puritan and didn't approve of Revere attending services there. Revere went to the West Church, now considered a US National Historic Landmark, where the phrase "no taxation without representation" was coined.

McCartney grew up with one younger brother, in Liverpool. He and his brother were baptized in their mother's Catholic faith, but their father was an agnostic; therefore, religion wasn't fully emphasized in their house. McCartney also auditioned to be a choirboy a St. Barnabas Parish Church, also a Church of England, located on Penny Lane. He actually failed his first two auditions to be in the church choir, claiming he failed one on purpose because he didn't want to be a choirboy.

These notable men were both **thirteen when their careers began**. At age thirteen, Paul Revere dropped out of school to become his father's apprentice as a silversmith. Being a silversmith helped Revere gain different connections to Boston society, which were useful when he became an active participant in the American Revolution. When Revere was nineteen, his father passed, but he was legally too young to take over his father's silver shop, so he joined the army as a second lieutenant. He stayed in the army for about a year until he moved back home, got married, and officially became the owner of his dad's silver shop.

At age thirteen, Paul McCartney met George Harrison, who he began making music with. As students, they both had impressively passed the eleven plus exam, gaining admission into prestigious grammar schools in Britain. They met on the bus on the way to the Liverpool Institute. By fifteen, McCartney and Harrison had been introduced to John Lennon and joined his band called The Quarrymen. Three years later, in 1960, they changed their name to The Beatles. By 1963, Ringo Starr had joined and the "Fab Four" was officially created.

Though Revere was talented with his silversmith artistry and McCartney is known as a talented musician, these men both have **multiple skills**. When Revere's business suffered during a recession, he casually took up dentistry in order to make more money. A practicing surgeon who was living at his friend's home taught him. Revere was also active in stonemasonry and served as a messenger for the Boston Committee of Public Safety, for which he delivered the message that the British were coming.

McCartney is also an accomplished painter. Over the years, he has had over seventy of his own paintings exhibited in the Walker Art Gallery in Liverpool, England. In addition to playing guitar, bass, and piano, McCartney's first instrument was the trumpet. He can also play the drums quite well.

Revere and McCartney can both be considered **activists**. Revere was one of the main leaders in the Boston Tea Party, when colonists dumped tea in protest to tea shipments that bypassed colonial merchants. He served on the Committee of Public Safety, which was a local committee of patriots performing as a shadow government that took control of the colonies.

McCartney is a vegetarian and an animal rights activist. He and his wife were vegetarians for most of their thirty-year marriage, and McCartney has continued their work since her death. They decided to stop eating meat after McCartney saw lambs in a field while they were eating lamb. He is a major supporter of the People for the Ethical Treatment of Animals organization. He has travelled to Prince Edward Island in Canada to raise international awareness of seal hunting and has debated politicians, stating that fishermen should stop hunting seals and start seal-watching businesses instead. McCartney has written to the Dalai Lama asking why he isn't a vegetarian. He supports Save the Arctic and narrated "Glass Walls," a video exploiting slaughterhouses, the meat industry, and animal welfare.

23

SANDRA DAY O'CONNOR TO SANDRA BULLOCK

Sandra Day O'Connor instantly became one of the most powerful role models for women when she was nominated by Ronald Reagan to sit on the Supreme Court. She served for twenty-four years, undergoing the challenge of battling breast cancer and her husband's suffering with Alzheimer's disease. She was a pioneering force on the Supreme Court and will be remembered as the guiding hand in the court's decisions during her time there, frequently acting as the swing vote. Sandra Bullock, also known as "America's sweetheart," is one of Hollywood's highest-paid actresses. She has starred in memorable movies such as *Miss Congeniality*, *The Blind Side*, *The Proposal*, and *Gravity*. She has received both an Academy Award and a Golden Globe Award. Most recently, in 2015, she was named "Most Beautiful Woman" by *People* magazine.

Sandra Day O'Connor and Sandra Bullock have both appeared in **Time magazine's "Time 100: The Most Influential People in the World."** O'Connor was named in the 2004 issue, being praised for her work in the Supreme Court. In *Time,* Walter Isaacson writes, "By being the practical-minded swing vote on the court, she has quietly become one of the most influential people in the world."

The 2010 *Time* list included Bullock, who is described by Betty White as a down-to-earth and genuinely kind person. In *Time,* White writes, "She never lets a scene get away from her. She's never just there going through her paces. And you can't take your eyes off of her. America, you wish she were your sweetheart."

O'Connor and Bullock are continuously recognized as **powerful women in their fields**. Several publications have named O'Connor one of the most powerful women in the world. As the swing vote in many Supreme Court cases, O'Connor had the opportunity to change history over and over again. And she did. In 2009, Obama awarded her the Presidential Medal of Freedom, which is the highest possible civilian honor one can be awarded in the United States.

The *Hollywood Reporter* named Bullock as one of the most powerful women in all of entertainment. By 2009, Bullock's films had grossed over $3.1 billion worldwide. Her total domestic gross stands at $1.7 billion, placing her among the Top 100 Stars at the Box Office. By 2014, she ranked number two on *Forbes* magazine's most powerful actresses list and was the highest earning actress in the movie business.

These two remarkable women each have their own connection to the state of **Texas**. O'Connor was born in El Paso, Texas and grew up on a ranch with her family. To honor her, a magnet school in Austin is named the Sandra Day O'Connor Criminal Justice/Public Service Academy. She also appears in the Texas Women's Hall of Fame.

Bullock, in addition to having a home in Lake Austin, Texas, actually owns her own restaurant in Austin called Bess Bistro. Across the street from her restaurant, she also opened Walton's Fancy and Staple, a bakery, upscale restaurant, flower shop, and an event planning business all in one. She backs a Texas non-profit organization called The Kindred Life Foundation, dedicated to helping individuals, households, and organizations in need.

It turns out, neither O'Connor nor Bullock has strict ties to a political party. They both have **democratic and republican views**. Though she is thought of as a conservative, O'Connor is also known for deciding her stance on a case-by-case basis. Willamette University College of Law professor Steven Green has stated, "She was a moderating voice on the court and was very hesitant to expand the law in either direction." He also said, unlike some other Court justices, O'Connor "seemed to look at each case with an open mind." Isn't that how it should be? Bullock, though she tries to keep her religious and political views private, has said she has "as many democratic ideas as she does republican."

Both Sandra Day O'Connor and Sandra Bullock have **completed firsts for women**. First, Sandra Day O'Connor was re-elected to the State Senate in 1973 and became the first woman to serve as majority leader. Next, President Ronald Reagan nominated her for a position as a Supreme Court justice, making her the first woman ever to hold that position. Sandra Bullock starred in *The Blind Side*, which broke box office records. She became the first female star to lead a film into the $200 million mark.

24

Scarlett O'Hara to Scarlett Johansson

When you hear the name Scarlett, odds are your mind probably jumps to either one of these beautiful women. Scarlett O'Hara is a famous leading character from the book *Gone With the Wind* by Margaret Mitchell, later adapted into a film. She's a spitfire, vain, and intelligent Southern belle, an uncommon protagonist.

Scarlett Johansson is a famous leading lady herself, starring in many movies and gracing the covers of countless magazines. She's an actress, model, and singer who is a sex symbol in Hollywood. She has done movies such as *Match Point*, *The Prestige*, *He's Just Not That Into You*, *The Avengers*, and *Her*. She has also released two music albums. Turns out, their name isn't the only thing they have in common.

Both women, at an early point in their lives, were **without much money**. O'Hara started out as a member of a wealthy family, but at the time of the Civil War, her whole world crashed and burned. She came close to starvation and homelessness when Sherman's army came through her hometown of

Georgia. Johansson has also claimed that, growing up, her family had very little money, and she attended a small public school in Manhattan.

Multiple sources say that Scarlett Johansson got her **name** from *Gone With the Wind*'s Scarlett O'Hara because her mother was a film buff who had dreams for her daughter to be an actress. Another interesting similarity is that Johansson's mother's name is Melanie, the same name as Scarlett O'Hara's BFF, Melanie Hamilton.

It also looks as though O'Hara and Johansson have had similar love lives. They both have had **multiple husbands** and marriages that haven't lasted too long. O'Hara first accepts the proposal from Melanie's brother, Charles Hamilton, who dies in the war. Next, she steals away her sister's fiancé, Frank Kennedy, in order to gain standing in his business and earn money for herself. Finally, husband number three is the illustrious and charming Rhett Butler, a man whom she really loves.

Johansson first married fellow actor Ryan Reynolds but the marriage only lasted two years. Now she's married to a French man named Romain Dauriac, with whom she had her first child, named Rose.

One cute little coincidence is that O'Hara and Johansson both have **daughters named after a color**. O'Hara's Bonnie Blue Butler was named such because of her bright blue eyes she inherited from Rhett. We can only guess that Rose was named as another word to describe the color red, just like her mother, Scarlett.

It goes without saying that these women have some kind of **sultry allure** that entices many men to adore them. In *Gone With the Wind*, we often see O'Hara surrounded by men who would be delighted to give her anything she wanted or even get the chance to exchange words with her.

Johansson is a major sex symbol in the media, being the only woman twice named the "Sexiest Woman Alive" by *Esquire* magazine. In addition, she has gained the title of "Sexiest Celebrity" by *Playboy* magazine.

O'Hara and Johansson are each known for their **clever personality**. Though both women have extremely good looks, their personalities don't suffer because of it. O'Hara isn't the typical Southern belle of her time. She has a quick wit that she uses to tease the men around her and only acts empty-headed or dainty when she needs to. O'Hara has a strong sense of self and doesn't shy away from taking what she wants. As for Johansson, she has also been described as much more than a pretty face and someone who has a great sense of humor. Woody Allen, who has worked with Johansson multiple times, once said about her that it is "very hard to be extra witty around a sexually overwhelming, beautiful young woman who is wittier than you are."

Scarlett O'Hara and Scarlett Johansson both seem to be beautiful, smart, and driven. Definitely two women to look up to!

25

Steve Jobs to Steve Carell

Steve Jobs is the mastermind behind the technology giant Apple Inc. and is considered a pioneer of the personal computer. He was an entrepreneur, marketer, and inventor with a legacy that will surely last. *Forbes* named him "the most powerful person in business in 2007". Jobs is a major role model and hero to anyone in the computer industry and is extremely respected for his work. Multiple biographies and films have been created to document his life and accomplishments. Steve Carell is an American actor, comedian, producer, director, and writer. He is best known for his role as Michael in the successful comedy series *The Office*, as well as his leading roles in movies such as *The 40-Year-Old Virgin*, *Get Smart*, *Despicable Me*, *The Way, Way Back*, *Crazy, Stupid Love*, and *Foxcatcher.* He was nominated as "America's funniest man" in *Life* magazine and received a Golden Globe for Best Actor in a Television Comedy Series for his role in *The Office*. Always funny, always talented, and always kind, Carell is one of the most lovable actors in Hollywood.

Steve Jobs and Steve Carell both grew up with **dads who were mechanics**. Jobs's dad, Paul Jobs, built a small workbench in their garage so he could teach his son about mechanics and pass along his love for it. Steve Jobs admired his dad's craftsmanship and watched him build things the family needed. He could build anything, from a new cabinet to a fence, and could fix a car, which Steve helped him with. We can probably guess that Steve Jobs got his drive for creation and computer science from his father. Steve Carell, on the other hand, had a dad who worked on the mechanics of computers. His dad was an electrical engineer.

Jobs and Carell have both **lived in California**. Jobs was born in San Francisco, right near Silicon Valley, which also influenced his interest in the up-and-coming computer industry. When he was in middle school, Jobs convinced his parents to move to Los Altos, California, to the home where the Apple Computer was first created. Once Jobs was married, he lived in Paolo Alto with his wife and children, the home where he passed away at the age of fifty-six due to his pancreatic cancer.

Carell was born in Massachusetts, went to school in Ohio, and performed with The Second City in Chicago. However, he found his current home, in Los Angeles, after becoming a successful actor and getting married. Carell currently resides in an estate within the Toluca Lake area.

Both of these men only got **married once,** in their mid-thirties. Jobs had a daughter named Lisa with his previous girlfriend, Chrisann Brennan, before marrying his wife, Laurene Powell, at age thirty-six. Jobs denied that he was the father of Lisa for years before finally admitting it to the public. It wasn't until he was forced out of the Apple Company and Lisa was seven years old that he started having a relationship with her. Jobs met his wife, Laurene, at a lecture series at Stanford Business School when the pair was seated next to each other. When she left at the conclusion of the lecture, Jobs ran after her and asked her out to dinner. With Laurene, Jobs had three more children: Reed, Erin, and Eve.

Carell met his wife, Nancy Walls, when she was a student in an improvisation class Carell was teaching at The Second City. They have worked together multiple times, with Nancy appearing in *The Daily Show*, *The Office*, and *The 40-Year-Old Virgin*, all of which Carell played a major role in. Nancy and Steve Carell have two children: Elisabeth and John.

Believe it or not, these two have both been involved with **Disney**. Steve Jobs bought The Graphics Group, now known as Pixar, in 1986. He orchestrated a deal with Disney, who bought Pixar for $7.4 billion. Jobs then became The Walt Disney Company's largest single shareholder, owning seven percent of their stock. He was also on the board of directors for The Walt Disney Company. In 2013, after Jobs's death, he was awarded the Disney Legends honor, given to those who have made great contributions to the company. Who knew? Carell might not own any stock or authority at Disney, but he has acted in multiple Disney productions. In 2014, he was Ben in the fantasy comedy *Alexander and the Terrible, Horrible, No Good, Very Bad Day*. He was also the voice of Mr. Delancey in Disney's animated series *Fillmore!* and starred in the film *Dan In Real Life*, which was distributed by Walt Disney Studios.

26

STEVEN SPIELBERG TO STEPHEN HAWKING

Steven Spielberg is an American director, producer, and screenwriter considered to be one of the founding pioneers of post-classical Hollywood. He's one of the most respected and influential directors and producers in all of film history, with a career that has lasted over four decades. He has directed some of the most famous films of all time, winning an Academy Award for Best Director for *Schindler's List* and *Saving Private Ryan*. Some other celebrated films of his are *Jaws*, *E.T. the Extra-Terrestrial*, *Jurassic Park*, and *Indiana Jones*. If you haven't seen any of those movies, you must be living under a rock.

Stephen Hawking is an English theoretical physicist and cosmologist, the world's most famous living scientist. He was the first to set forth the theory of cosmology, by combining Einstein's general theory of relativity and quantum mechanics. His book, *A Brief History of Time*, was a bestseller and explained large topics in cosmology, such as the big bang, black holes, and light cones, to the average reader. He has been awarded the Presidential Medal of Freedom, the highest civilian award in the United States. Hawking suffers from rare, early-onset amyotrophic lateral sclerosis (ALS). The disease started to affect him in grad school and has slowly progressed, paralyzing him to the point where Hawking must now communicate using a single cheek muscle attached to a speech-generating device.

You probably wouldn't have guessed it, but Spielberg and Hawking were not good students. They both **did poorly in school**. Spielberg got interested in movie making at a very young age, making his first home movie at age twelve. He continued to make amateur "adventure" films as a boy and won a prize for a 40-minute war film titled *Escape to Nowhere* that he made at age thirteen. At sixteen, he wrote and directed his first independent film that was 140 minutes long and was a science fiction adventure titled *Firelight*. He wanted to become a film director and applied to the University of Southern California's film school, only to be denied due to his C grade average. Looks like Spielberg spent a lot of time movie making and very little time studying. He ended up getting admitted to California State University in Long Beach and majored in English. As a college student, he got an unpaid internship at Universal Studios, which was so impressed with him that they offered Spielberg a seven-year directing contract. He was the youngest director ever signed for a long-term contract with a major Hollywood Studio.

Stephen Hawking was similar with his lack of studying as boy and was a known slacker when it came to schoolwork. When he was nine, he actually ranked among the worst in his class. Despite the poor grades, teachers and peers recognized his genius ability, and he earned the nickname "Einstein." Young Hawking was interested in mathematics, but his father urged him to instead pursue a career in medicine because there were few jobs for math graduates. At seventeen, he ended up studying physics and chemistry at University College, Oxford, which he found painfully easy, and he hardly ever studied. That must be nice, huh? After acing his exams, he went to get his PhD at Cambridge, where he was first diagnosed with ALS.

Spielberg and Hawking both have had **two wives**. Spielberg met his first wife when she was suggested as a possible actress for the movie he was working on, called *Close Encounters*. After they met, he told his friend, "I met a real heartbreaker last night." She didn't get the role in his movie because she was too young, but she and Spielberg did begin dating. They dated for four years before breaking up. Five years later, they reconnected and got married, already having a son together named Max Samuel. They were married for three and a half years, but rivaling stresses over their careers led them to divorce. Spielberg met his second wife, Kate Capshaw, after casting her in *Indiana Jones and the Temple of Doom*. Capshaw converted from Protestantism to Judaism for Spielberg, who is Jewish. They had three kids together and adopted two more. They're still happily married and split time between their four homes in NY, California, and Florida.

Stephen Hawking met fellow grad student Jane Wilde at Cambridge, shortly before his ALS diagnosis. Hawking lapsed into depression with the news and has said his engagement to Jane "gave him something to live for." They had three children together and were married for thirty years. Following strains on their marriage and Hawking becoming somewhat of a celebrity, Hawking left Jane for his nurse, Elaine Mason. They were married eleven years before divorcing quietly. Hawking has sense resumed a closer relationship with Jane, his children, and his grandchildren.

Their impactful influences in their fields as primary examples of excellence led them to both receive **honorary degrees and awards**. Spielberg has been recognized by and awarded a degree from Boston University, Brown University, University of Southern California, and Yale University. He also has won three Academy Awards and was honored as an honorary Knight Commander of the Order of the British Empire by Queen Elizabeth II. Hawking apparently declined to be knighted, but he has received twelve honorary degrees, including one from the University of Oxford. He has been awarded further academic recognition by receiving the prestigious Albert Einstein Medal for his scientific discoveries related to Albert Einstein.

27

Thomas Edison to Tom Hanks

Thomas Edison is one of the most famous American inventors, recognized for developing many world-changing devices, including the phonograph, the motion picture camera, and, of course, the light bulb. February 11, Thomas Edison's birthday, is National Inventor's Day, designated by the US Congress.

Thomas "Tom" Hanks is one of the most respected and well-liked American actors, known for his roles in films such as *Forrest Gump*, *Saving Private Ryan*, *Sleepless in Seattle*, *Cast Away*, *The Da Vinci Code*, and *Captain Phillips*. He has won numerous awards during his career, including multiple Golden Globes and Academy Awards and the Kennedy Center Honors Medallion. As of 2014, Hanks's films have grossed over $8.4 billion worldwide, making him one of the highest-grossing actors in film history.

These guys both know what it's like to grow up with a big family. Edison and Hanks were both **one of seven**. Edison, his mother's favorite son, grew up in a crowded home with six other siblings. Edison was the youngest and also the smartest of the bunch, eager to learn even with his undiagnosed ADHD. Hanks grew up as one of four, with three brothers and one sister. His parents got divorced when he was only four years old. When he was in high school, his father remarried, and he gained three new stepsiblings, bringing the total to seven.

These two are obviously very successful individuals, but it turns out they weren't so successful socially. Thomas Edison and Tom Hanks were **not popular in school**. Edison's head was oddly larger than average, and he donned a noticeably broad forehead. As a young student, his moderately unusual demeanor and appearance, as well as his wandering mind, made him somewhat of an outcast. At age seven, after only three months of schooling, Edison's teacher lost his patience with the persistent questioning and self-centered nature of the boy. Edison was homeschooled for the rest of his education by his mother. Poor guy!

When Hanks is asked about his early childhood, he doesn't remember it too fondly. He was unpopular with teachers and students. Hanks claims he didn't have too many friends, and he once told *Rolling Stone* in an interview, "I was a geek, a spaz. I was horribly, painfully, terribly shy. At the same time, I was the guy who'd yell out funny captions during filmstrips. But I didn't get into trouble. I was always a real good kid and pretty responsible." It looks like if we went to school with either of these guys when we were young, we probably would've avoided them.

Before Edison and Hanks were famous, they both **sold food as a kid to earn money**. Edison worked on a train in Michigan, running from the city of Port Huron to Detroit as a young boy. He sold candy and newspapers and occasionally vegetables to passengers to supplement his income. As a teenager in California, Hanks worked at the Oakland Coliseum and sold concessions at A's and Raiders games.

Believe it or not, both Edison and Hanks had **dreams of becoming an actor** and had a **love for Shakespeare**. Edison's father urged Edison to read all of the classics, giving him ten cents for every one he completed. Because of this, Edison gained a great appreciation for literature, especially Shakespeare. His fondness for Shakespeare's plays even lead him to briefly consider becoming an actor. However, his high-pitched voice and his extreme shyness before every audience led him to give up the idea.

Hanks became a fan of acting at a young age, attending many different plays. As he grew older, he liked to make a lot of noise and be flamboyantly outgoing, so he turned to acting as a career. Hanks studied theater at Chabot College for two years, then at California State University. Hanks acted in multiple Shakespeare plays, such as his first professional performance in *The Two Gentlemen of Verona*, and he was a member of Riverside Shakespeare Company.

New York City is the place where Edison and Hanks started moving up in their careers. After inventing the phonograph, Edison looked toward electricity and the light bulb. He formed the Edison Electric Light Company, now known as General Electric (GE), in New York City. It was after creating this company that he successfully invented an electric lamp and made the first public demonstration of his incandescent light bulb on December 31, 1879, in Menlo Park. During this time, he is quoted saying, "We will make electricity so cheap that only the rich will burn candles."

At age twenty-three, Hanks moved to NYC where he made his film debut, funnily enough, in a slasher movie entitled *He Knows You're Alone*. After moving to New York in 1979, he also got roles in television shows, a game show, and other small movies. It wasn't until 1988 with his starring role in *Big* that Hanks solidified his career as a major Hollywood talent.

Edison and Hanks were both **married twice**. When Edison was twenty-four, he married sixteen-year-old Mary Stilwell. She was an employee in one of his shops. They had three children together before she died at age twenty-nine from a brain tumor. He remarried at age thirty-nine to twenty-year-old Mina Miller. They also had three children together. They remained married until Edison's death in 1931.

Hanks got married to American actress Samantha Lewes when he was twenty-two. The marriage lasted nine years, and they had two children together, Colin and Elizabeth. One year after their separation, Hanks married actress Rita Wilson, whom he met filming *Volunteers*, a movie they costarred in together. Hanks and Rita have been married twenty-seven years and have two sons, Chet and Truman Theodore.

These men may not have lived in the same time period, but they both have been involved in **filmmaking**. One of Edison's inventions is, in fact, a motion picture camera or the "kinetograph." He made an electromechanical design and a peephole viewer, or a "kinetoscope," which allowed people to watch short, simple films. It made its first debut in 1891. By 1896, New York City was projecting motion pictures in public screenings.

Hanks may not have actually invented the technology to make films, but he has played a part in creating the films themselves. He made his directing debut with his 1996 film, *That Thing You Do!* Next, he executive produced, co-wrote, and co-directed the HBO docudrama *From the Earth to the Moon*. Him and his wife, Rita, produced the hit film, *My Big Fat Greek Wedding.* He is most known for his involvement with legendary Stephen Spielberg to create one of the finest war films ever made, *Saving Private Ryan.*

One fun little fact is that **President Abraham Lincoln** connects these men. Lincoln was president during Thomas Edison's lifetime, being elected in 1861 when Edison was fourteen years old. Tom Hanks is actually a fourth cousin, four generations removed, of Abraham Lincoln, of all people. What a cool relative to have!

28

Tina Turner to Tina Fey

Tina Turner is most successful in her career as a singer, termed the most successful female rock artist ever. She's listed in the *Guinness Book of Records* for selling more concert tickets than any solo performer in history. You've probably heard some of her most famous songs, such as "What's Love Got to Do with It," "Private Dancer," "Let's Stay Together," and her rendition of "Proud Mary." She is the winner of eight Grammy Awards and has sold around 200 million records worldwide. If Tina Turner is called the "Queen of Rock n' Roll," then Tina Fey can be called the "Queen of Comedy." Fey has received eight Emmys, two Golden Globes, five Screen Actors Guild Awards, and four Writers Guild of America Awards for her work. Within the comedy field, she's considered to be one of the best, and she still continues to be a trailblazing woman comedian. She is well-known for her work in the *Saturday Night Live* (*SNL*) series, being the creator of the critically acclaimed show *30 Rock* and performing as an actress in multiple, wildly successful films.

Tina Turner and Tina Fey weren't always named Tina; in fact, they both were **born with different names.** Tina Turner was born Anna Mae Bullock in 1939. It was her husband, Ike Turner, who thought of the name change to "Tina," because it rhymed with television character "Sheena" from the comic book *Sheena, Queen of the Jungle*. It's believed that Ike renamed twenty-one-year-old Anna Mae Bullock because he didn't want her to run off and make a name for herself. Later, Ike admitted that another reason for the name change was to keep Tina's former lovers from returning to her. Tina Fey was born Elizabeth Stamatina Fey. "Tina" is taken from the latter part of her middle name. Fey changed her name for purely aesthetic reasons.

These famous ladies knew they were destined for stardom from the beginning and **started becoming interested in their future careers at a very young age.** Turner realized she had a talent for singing and became a member of Nutbush's Spring Hill Baptist Church choir as a child. Barely in her teens, high schooler Turner quickly immersed herself in St. Louis's R&B scene, spending much of her time at Club Manhattan with her older sister. It was there, in 1956, that she met rock-and-roll pioneer Ike Turner, band member of the Kings of Rhythm. Few women had ever sung with him, but it wasn't long before Turner was performing with the group, quickly becoming the highlight of their show.

Tina Fey was introduced to comedy by her parents at a young age and grew up watching *Saturday Night Live*, Monty Python, *Second City Television*, and old Marx Brothers movies. By age eleven, she had already read *Seventy Years of Great Film Comedians* by Joe Franklin for a school project about comedy. As a teenager, she knew she was interested in comedy. By high school, she was taking drama classes and writing consistently. It was Fey's eighth grade teacher who encouraged her to be a writer. To *People* magazine, Fey said originally, she thought, "I don't want to be a writer, 'cause then you're just by yourself in a room all the time. I want to be a star!" After earning a degree in drama from the University of Virginia, she moved to Chicago to start her comedy career at The Second City.

Both women found success while performing on none other than the famously hilarious late-night sketch comedy and variety show, **Saturday Night Live (SNL)**. Tina Turner, in her first solo act ever, performed at The Ritz in NYC in 1981. Rod Stewart noticed her and, following that performance, asked her to join him on *SNL* to perform a duet of his song "Hot Legs." This performance brought her recognition and the beginning of her fame, and Stewart later hired Turner to open for him on his US tour.

In comparison, Tina Fey got her break-out role on *SNL* and is still considered one of the most famous *SNL* cast members of all time. Fey worked at *SNL* for nine years before starting her career developing her hit show *30 Rock*. In 2015, in *Rolling Stone Magazine*'s appraisal of all 141 *SNL* cast members to date, Fey was ranked as number three in importance, right behind John Belushi and Eddie Murphy. Fey was also *SNL*'s first female head writer.

These beautiful women didn't have to go looking for a husband because they both **married men they worked with**. Tina Turner found Ike Turner as a teenager at Club Manhattan. After joining his band, the Kings of Rhythm, and starting their own duo, Ike & Tina Turner Revue, the couple's success was picking up pace, and they married in 1962. By the mid-1970s, their marriage had fallen apart due to Ike's cocaine addiction, frequent infidelity, and physical abuse of Tina. She is currently married to her second husband, German music executive Erwin Bach, whom she met at a record label party in London in 1985. Tina Fey found love two years into her career at The Second City in Chicago with the show's piano player turned musical director, Jeff Richmond. They are still married and live with their two daughters in NYC.

Turner and Fey aren't one-trick ponies, for both of them **have succeeded in multiple fields**. In addition to being a famous singer, Turner has also experienced success in films, including a role in the 1975 rock musical *Tommy* and a starring role in the 1985 Mel Gibson blockbuster film, *Mad Max*

Beyond Thunderdome, as well as a cameo role in the 1993 film *Last Action Hero.* Tina is also known as a very good dancer and choreographer. With her success as an entertainer who can act, sing, and dance, Tina Turner is a triple threat.

Tina Fey, in addition to being a respected and highly regarded comedian, is an actress, writer, and producer. Along with being a head writer for *SNL*, Fey was the creator, executive producer, writer, and star of the show *30 Rock.* Over the course of the series, the show was nominated for 112 Emmy Awards and won sixteen, in addition to numerous other nominations and wins from other awards shows. Fey has also acted in multiple movies, including the successful teen comedy *Mean Girls*, which she also wrote. Fey teamed up with her BFF, Amy Poehler, for *Baby Mama*, which grossed over $64 million at the box office. Next she costarred with Steve Carell in the 2010 comedy *Date Night* and has acted other successful films.

You know you've made it when you can write a book about yourself and have it become a bestseller. Both Tina Turner and Tina Fey **wrote successful autobiographies**. Turner's book, entitled *I, Tina*, describes the story of young girl born in Tennessee who rises to fame after meeting Ike Turner. She describes their abusive relationship that ended before she became an international superstar. The book, after being published in 1986, became a worldwide best-seller and led to the film adaption, *What's Love Got to Do with It*.

Fey's autobiography, the hilarious *Bossypants*, gives her life story as to how she became a member of *SNL* and what she went through to create *30 Rock*. Her book topped *The New York Times* Best Seller List and stayed there for five straight weeks upon its release in 2011. The book has sold over one million copies in the US, and Fey's narration of the audiobook was Grammy nominated.

29

WALT WHITMAN TO WALT DISNEY

Walt Whitman, sometimes called "America's Poet," was a poet, essayist and journalist. Whitman was also a humanist, often reflecting on the value and agency of human beings. He incorporated both transcendentalism and realism into his work. Transcendentalism being the spirituality and inherent goodness of people, and realism being the focus on people's everyday actions, lacking romanticized presentation. His major work is *Leaves of Grass*, published in 1855 with his own money. The poetry collection was considered quite controversial during the time he was alive because of its obscenity and overt sexuality. He spent the rest of his life expanding and revising it.

Walt Disney is the American cartoonist and animator who became a cultural icon with the creation of characters including Mickey Mouse, Donald Duck, and Goofy. Disney himself was the original voice for Mickey and came up with the idea for the theme parks. He has won twenty-two Academy Awards from fifty-nine nominations, giving him more Academy Awards and nominations than any other person in history.

Though they moved on to bigger and better things, Whitman and Disney started out in the **newspaper business**. Whitman's first job after finishing his formal schooling at age eleven was as an apprentice and printer's devil for the weekly *Long Island Patriot* newspaper. He learned about the printing press, typesetting, and writing. The next summer, he worked for the *Long-Island Star*, a Whig weekly newspaper, and started anonymously publishing his earliest poetry in the *New York Mirror* newspaper. He even started his own newspaper called the *Long Islander*, of which he was the publisher, editor, pressman, and distributor.

When Disney was eleven, his father purchased a news-paper delivery route for *The Kansas City Star*, and young Walt and his brother were put to work delivering them. They delivered the morning paper, *Kansas City Times*, to about 700 customers. The evening paper and the Sunday paper were delivered to more than 600. The number of customers they delivered to increased over time. Little Walt woke up at 4:30 a.m. and delivered newspapers until his first class at school began, and then he resumed the paper trail after school at 4 p.m. until dinnertime. He did this for six years, constantly exhausted and receiving poor grades for falling asleep during class.

These men were both storytellers who **could paint a picture**. Whitman's *Leaves of Grass* poetry collection is known for its heavily descriptive wording, allowing the reader to visualize the scene he was describing. From rotting leaves to tufts of straw, he paints the picture for the reader, such as "the beautiful uncut hair of graves." He used imagery to bring the audience to the scene. Whitman especially paid attention to sounds with a stream-of-consciousness effect of someone looking around at the world around him. "Song of Myself," an epic poem in *Leaves of Grass*, is thought to be comparable to Homer's works, such as the *Iliad* and the *Odyssey*.

Walt Disney painted a picture through his cartoons. Mickey Mouse was actually based on a mouse he had as a pet during his early career at Laugh-O-Gram studio in Kansas City. The first animated short with Disney's Mickey was called *Plane Crazy* and was a silent film. This film also featured Minnie. Mickey is building his own airplane, and Minnie gives him a horseshoe for good luck. Shortly after, Disney created *Steamboat Willie* with sound, and it quickly became a success. After this, Mickey was the world's most popular cartoon character.

These icons both **died due to lung problems**. In 1892, Walt Whitman passed away. An autopsy showed that he had bronchial pneumonia but died from pleurisy, military tuberculosis, and parenchymatous nephritis. That's a lot of big words! Basically, his lungs had been reduced to one-eighth of their normal breathing volume. There was also inflammation of the lining surrounding his lungs and sores throughout his lungs. At the public viewing of his body during the funeral proceedings, over one thousand people came to see Whitman, and his coffin was hard to see because it was so completely surrounded by flowers people had left for him.

Walt Disney was unfortunately a chain smoker during his life as an adult, but he made sure children never saw him with a cigarette in his mouth. During the X-rays before going in for a surgery for an old neck injury, Disney's doctors found a tumor in his left lung. The tumor was cancerous and had spread throughout his whole lung. Disney's lung was removed, and he was told his life expectancy was anywhere between six months to two years. The month after removing his lung, Disney died of circulatory collapse due to his lung cancer. The last Disney productions he was involved in before his death were *The Jungle Book*, *The Happiest Millionaire*, and *Winnie the Pooh and the Blustery Day*. An urban legend remains that Disney's body was frozen and lies beneath the Pirates of the Caribbean ride at Disneyland, but the reality is that Disney's remains were cremated, and his ashes were spread at the Forest Lawn Memorial Park in California.

30

WILLIAM SHAKESPEARE TO WILL FERRELL

William Shakespeare is a playwright and poet, considered to be the greatest writer in the English language of all time. He's written 38 plays, 154 sonnets, and 2 long narrative poems. His plays have been translated into every major language and are performed more than those of any other playwright in history. Many of his play's expressions are now used in everyday speech, such as "catch a cold," "green-eyed monster," "the world is your oyster," "love is blind," "wild goose chase," "heart of gold," "wear your heart on your sleeve," and "method to his madness," just to name a few.

Will Ferrell might not have shaped the English language, but he sure has shaped the way for modern comedy. Ferrell is an American actor, comedian, producer, and writer. He's included as a member of leading Hollywood comic actors and is frequently listed as one of the funniest people alive. He is known for his work on *Saturday Night Live* and hilarious films such as *Anchorman*, *Talladega Nights*, *Blades of Glory*, *Step Brothers*, and *The Other Guys*. Ferrell also launched the successful "Funny or Die" streaming video site for short comedy films.

Shakespeare wasn't always behind the curtain. He and Will Ferrell are actually both **actors**. William Shakespeare's plays started being performed on stage in 1592, and he immediately began gaining recognition as a talented playwright. Before building his famous Globe Theatre, Shakespeare and a small group of men owned a company called Lord Chamberlain's Men. They became the leading playing company in London. Shakespeare continued to act in his own plays and others, even as his fame and success as a playwright grew. It is believed that Shakespeare played the ghost of Hamlet's father, Adam, in *As You Like It* and was a chorus member in *Henry V*.

Will Ferrell is known well for his work as an actor, starring in many memorable comedy films that have made him a household name. After becoming a member of the comedy group The Groundlings and landing a spot as a cast member on *Saturday Night Live*, Will Ferrell started his movie acting career by appearing in small roles, before landing his first starring role in *Old School* and then *Elf.*

So we know Shakespeare acted in his own plays, but it's also true that both of these men **starred in their own productions**. In fact, Ferrell's biggest accomplishments as an actor came from films he was involved in making. In 2010, Ferrell was the executive producer and star of the film *The Other*

Guys, alongside Mark Wahlberg. The buddy cop film was a box office success, earning over $140 million. Ferrell was a writer for his movie *Anchorman*, in which he was the star. The film is considered one of Ferrell's greatest movies. A sequel was made nine years later, and there is even talk of a third *Anchorman* to be produced at a later date. Another victorious film of Ferrell's, and a movie he is also well known for, is *Step Brothers*. Ferrell wrote the screenplay and the story for the film as well as played the starring role alongside John C. Reilly. The film is rumored to have a sequel in the works.

These successful men both made time for their family and had **three children**. Shakespeare, at the age of eighteen, married twenty-six-year-old Anne Hathaway. She was three months pregnant at the time of their marriage. Six months after the marriage, the couple had a daughter named Susana, followed two years later by a set of twins named Hamnet and Judith. Hamnet died of unknown causes at age eleven. Ferrell married a Swedish actress named Viveca Paulin in 2000. Ferrell met Paulin in an acting class in 1995. They have homes in New York City and Orange County, California. Ferrell has three sons with Paulin: Magnus, Mattias, and Axel.

If Shakespeare and Ferrell ever met, they'd be sure to have a **sense of humor** in common. Shakespeare's famous comedies have produced some of the very beginnings of comedy. "Knock, knock! Who's there?" we actually owe to

Shakespeare, along with the phrases like "break the ice," "laughing stock," and "in a pickle." Shakespeare was a fan of parodies, often using his plays to parody his acting company and the relationships between the writers, directors, and actors. He also enjoyed puns, making the title of *Much Ado About Nothing* a pun. The play is a comedy of misunderstandings and of characters trying to make sense of each other and the world. The characters make much out of unimportant situations, therefore much over nothing. Get it?

Ferrell might have a different take on humor, but he is definitely another important comedian. "What I recognized when I started doing comedy was that I'm probably not the wittiest, not the fastest on my feet, but the one thing I can guarantee is that I won't hold anything back," Ferrell explained to *Esquire* magazine. When he was part of *Saturday Night Live*'s cast, Ferrell was the first choice when writing a new sketch. Ferrell was selected as the 2011 recipient of the Mark Twain Prize for American Humor.

Even though Shakespeare was a play actor, and Ferrell's a movie actor, these two actors have both **performed in plays**. Ferrell made his Broadway debut with his performances as George W. Bush, someone he imitated frequently on *SNL*, in a one-man show called *You're Welcome America. A Final Night with George W. Bush*. Ferrell wrote the play, and its first preview performance began on January 20, 2009, Bush's final day in office. The play opened officially on February 1 and was performed through March 15. It was broadcast live on HBO on March 14 and was nominated for a Tony Award for Best Special Theatrical Event.

About the Author

Molly Mae Force is currently a student at the University of Michigan graduating in 2017. She's a double major in English and Communications. She recently completed an internship with Networlding Publishing Inc. in Chicago and has also had an internship as a paid reporter for the Detroit Free Press. Her first internship was a blogger for the Oakland Press. As a high school student, she won the Yale Book Award for her excellence in English language and literature. Her senior class superlative was 'Most Hipster.' She's a member of Michigan's Quidditch Team and is proud to be a nerdy Harry Potter fan. She's also a member of the Michigan Marching Band and plays the alto saxophone. Molly spent two months in Italy for a study abroad trip learning Italian and adored getting lost in Venice. Her first book was called "Molly's Party" which she wrote in first grade. It was about her dream birthday party that featured Clifford the Big Red

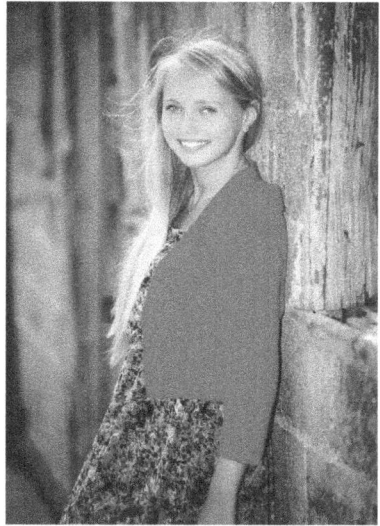

Dog and a waterslide. The bounders of the book messed up her name and put "Molly Moe Force" on the cover. Her parents got a good laugh out of that. When she's not living in Ann Arbor, she lives with her mom, dad, and beagle in Birmingham, Michigan.

Want More?

If you enjoyed this book check out the series that includes:

- Masters Mashups: From Marie Antoinette to Madonna

- Masters Mashups: Princess Grace to Princess Kate

- Masters Mashups: Shakespeare to Stephen King

- Mashups for Teens: Sleeping Beauty to Beyoncé